Handbook for Counseling Girls and Women

Volume 2

Talent Development

Ten Years of Research from the National Science Foundation Gender Equity Projects at Arizona State University

Barbara Kerr, Ph.D.
Sharon E. Robinson Kurpius, Ph.D.
Amy Harkins, M.C.
Editors

First U.S. Edition March, 2005
Second U.S. Printing June, 2005

Library of Congress Control Number: 2005922671

ISBN 0974767727

1. Science 2. Psychology 3. Gender Studies

Cover Image and Graphics: Kirsten Sorensen

Published by Nueva Science Press
A division of MTR Worldwide, LLC
1814 North 74th Place
Mesa, Arizona 85207
480 629 5977

Printed in the United States of America

NUEVA
SCIENCE

Acknowledgments

There are many people we would like to thank for helping us bring these projects to fruition. First, we would like to thank all of the wonderful female doctoral students in counseling psychology at ASU who served as research assistants and worked so closely with the adolescent girls and young women involved in TARGETS, GEMS, or GEOS. Christine Trainer Haas, Julie Beasley, Laurie Burke, Corrisa Chopp, Katherine Vaughn Fielder, Abby Garcia, Maria Darcy, Andrea Brown, Laura Huser, Megan Foley Nicpon, Sarah Lowery, Camea Gagliardi, and Natasha Maynard-Reid were devoted to making these projects successful and through their effors, these projects came to life. In addition, we want to thank all of the counseling and counseling psychology students who became involved in the numerous research projects and conference presentation that evolved from our work with these adolescent girls and young women. Much more is known about talent, at-risk behaviors, and resiliency among adolescent girls and young women because of the research studies of Christine Trainer Haas, Leticia Amick-Lofton, Elva Hull Blanks, Corissa Chopp, Abby Garcia, Katherine Vaughn Fielder, Sarah Hart, Alison Toren, Teissy Meza, and Sarah Lowery. We also want to thank three male doctoral students—Tim Davis, Troy Melendez, and Jessie Garcia—who expanded our programs to conduct similar interventions with adolescent boys and young men. Finally, we want to thank the many counseling and counseling psychology students who devoted many Fridays to this project as volunteers. Very special appreciation goes to Amy Harkins, Nan Benally, Debbiesiu Lee, Sandra

Dannenbaum, and Margaret Corrigan who spent many Fridays helping to make these projects successful when we were short of counselors and needed someone to help at the last minute. We could always count of these women unselfishly giving of their time and expertise so that the adolescent girls and women would benefit from these projects. We want to thank our colleagues at ASU who recognized and respected our passion for working with the girls and women involved in TARGETS, GEMS, or GEOS. Your support was always appreciated. We thank John McAlister of Nueva Science /MTR for publishing our book and Kirsten Sorensen for cover design. Finally, we want to thank Ruta Sevo and Lola Rogers for recognizing the importance of our proposed work and supporting our work through the National Science Foundation.

Dedication

To every talented girl and woman who has shared her hopes and dreams with us.

- The Research Team

Table of Contents

Section 3: Impact of TARGETS and GEOS: Research Findings

Introduction
Talent Development Handbook
Barbara Kerr

The second volume of *Counseling Girls and Women, Talent Development* is intended as a research and practice guide to the assessment, individual counseling, and group counseling strategies that were developed by the National Science Foundation sponsored gender equity projects at Arizona State University. The two major programs were Talented At Risk Girls: Encouragement and Training for Sophomores (TARGETS) and Gender Equity Options in Science (GEOS). The objectives of both programs were the enhancement of self-esteem and self-efficacy as well as the encouragement of choices that would promote participants' chances of persisting in their career goals. Although our focus was on the guidance of mathematically and scientifically talented girls and women, we carefully developed these techniques so that they would be generalizable to all females who aspire to nontraditional goals. Our focus with high school age girls was overcoming those barriers that impeded interest and ability in persisting in long term career goals, entering college, and leading balanced lives. With college women, our emphasis was on overcoming challenges to persisting in college, holding fast to career dreams, and surviving in challenging college majors.

Volume One of *Counseling Girls and Women* explored the factors that created risks in the lives of high school girls and college women and the factors that promoted resiliency. The section on ethnicity explored in depth the unique challenges faced by talented girls and women in each major American ethnic group. A section on risk behaviors investigated the ways adolescent girls and college women negotiate the constraints of gender role socialization while attempting to develop their talents. Finally, a section on protective factors described those internal and external conditions that seemed to provide the capacity for talented girls and women to resist gender role stereotypes and the pressure to compromise their dreams.

Volume Two of *Counseling Girls and Women* provides an introduction to the course of talent development in adolescent girls and college women. Chapter One reviews the ways in which changing societal expectations of adolescent girls have affected the ways in which bright girls respond to their own talents. Sex differences in achievement, aspirations, personality, and interests emerge as a result of the different ways in which girls and boys are taught to view the value and the possibilities of their gifts. Girls are indeed increasing their achievement in math and science and their leadership in educational and vocational activities. It appears, however, that the closing of the gender gap is not without its costs, as can be seen in Chapter Two, where

9

the difficulties and ambiguities of college life for talented girls and women are described. This chapter emphasizes as well the problems encountered by women who choose nontraditional majors in science, technology, engineering and math and the factors that affect persistence in these areas.

The second section of this volume is a detailed explanation of the techniques used in the TARGETS and GEOS programs for career and personal guidance. A typical day at a TARGETS workshop is explained through the eyes of a participant. The use of value-based activities such as the Rokeach Values Inventory and the Perfect Future Day Fantasy activity are described in the next chapter. Both of the major personality assessment instruments used in the workshops, the Vocational Preference Inventory and the Personality Research Form are described in the next chapters, with analyses of the profiles associated with various vocational orientations and personality patterns of talented girls and women.

The third section of this volume will be of interest to evaluators, researchers, and those counselors who are searching for empirically based techniques for counseling young women. An outcome study of the TARGETS program showed that the counseling strategies employed by the program had clear immediate and long term effects on the girl's perceptions of themselves and the career behaviors. The study of the GEOS interventions had similar findings, with the additional hopeful conclusion that these techniques may truly be able to help talented young women to hold fast to their aspirations and plans. A final qualitative evaluation of the GEOS program brings the young women alive in the narratives of their experiences with the mentoring, the faculty student retreat, and the counseling program.

We hope that this second volume will allow other counselors in high schools and colleges to replicate our work. The resources required are a willing group of counselors or mentor volunteers; access to the psychological instruments we use, which any certified counselor can order; a place to gather girls together that is friendly and warm; and plenty of snacks! With the first and second volumes of this series, our hope is that counselors and the educators who provide guidance will have learned about the special needs of talented at risk adolescent girls; the barriers to persistence toward nontraditional career goals; and the ways of helping girls overcome those barriers.

Section 1

Talent Development

In order to create interventions for talented girls and women, it is important to understand the ways in which their talents emerge, differentiate, and develop. In addition, counselors must understand how female talent development differs from that of males. The first chapter in this section describes how bright girls differ from bright boys in their development, academic achievement, psychological adjustment, and career aspirations. Their socialization and schooling is examined, with special emphasis on how self-beliefs are formed and how classroom and societal inequities shape girls' performance and goals. The second chapter continues with the development of talented college women. The special challenges of the college environment include the "culture of romance" and the discouragement in science, technology, engineering and math. Support, role models, and mentoring are shown to be critical to both academic persistence and career goal attainment.

1

The Development of Talent in Girls and Young Women

Barbara Kerr
Megan Foley-Nicpon
Angela L. Zapata

For the last twenty years in the U.S., girls have begun to close the gender gap with boys in many ways. Eighth grade girls have caught up with boys in math achievement, despite the researchers' predictions that biological differences would preclude girls from the highest attainments in mathematics (NCES, 2003). Bright girls enter challenging biology, chemistry, and physics classes in almost the same numbers as bright boys. Efforts aimed at helping girls to raise their career aspirations, to attempt more rigorous course work, and to claim leadership positions have been successful. The number of gifted women who plan careers in medicine, law, and many other fields that were once dominated by men is now equal to that of gifted men (Campbell & Clewell, 1999). Girls now hold approximately 80% of high school leadership positions, and girls' and women's athletics have captured the nation's attention.

As girls and women become more active in traditionally male domains, they often take on the problems that males have experienced: substance abuse, violence, and self-destructiveness (Phillips, 1998). Along with these newly acquired difficulties, girls and women continue to struggle with societal expectations of the "perfect" woman, and attempt to attain impossible ideals of physical beauty. Ninety percent of people with eating disorders, which have the highest mortality rate of any mental illness, are women (National Institute of Mental Health, 1993).

Internal and external barriers to attaining goals still exist for gifted women (Leroux, 1994). Gifted women are excluded from colleges and academic opportunities due to lower achievement test scores. The gender gap in math achievement at the highest range of scores has not changed (Campbell & Clewell, 1999). College women continue to endure a virulent culture of romance that forces them into competition for relationships with high prestige males (Holland & Eisenhart, 1990). The culture of romance is a socialization strategy that relies on women's reproductive roles (Firestone, 1970). In the workplace, women often find that discrimination is subtle, and includes barriers such as the dearth of childcare, inflexible scheduling, and lack of mentoring. Young professional women's partners often do not support their ambitions or goals; and as a result, these women may compromise their dreams in an attempt to maintain a lifestyle that works for their families (Tomlinson-Keasey, 1999).

The conflicts between gender identity and achievement motivation that gifted girls and women experience can prevent them from attaining the education they need to follow through on career goals, as well as from forming satisfying and health relationships. The development of talent in girls and women is often hindered by social pressures to attain ideals of femininity. With an understanding of gender and giftedness, counselors can help to guide young women through the critical "milestones and danger zones" of gender socialization that threaten the fulfillment of their talent.

Differences and Similarities between Gifted Girls and Gifted Boys

Developmental Differences - Giftedness is evident in girls at an earlier age than boys; gifted girls are more likely to show developmental advancement in a variety of areas (Silverman, 1986). Gifted girls are likely to speak, read, and write earlier than gifted boys. Though girls with a high IQ tend to be taller, stronger, and healthier than girls of average IQ (Terman & Oden, 1935), they may feel less physically competent than gifted boys (Chan, 1988).

Gifted boys are taller, stronger, and healthier than average boys (Terman & Oden, 1935). Large muscle development occurs earlier and, therefore, gifted boys are more active and physically competent than gifted girls (Kerr & Cohn, 2001). However, gifted boys are likely to be less advanced in language development and less likely to be precocious readers than gifted girls (Silverman, 1986).

Ability and Achievement - Gifted girls outperform gifted boys in classroom achievement throughout the school years, maintaining higher grades in all subjects (Gallagher, 1985). However, this underperformance may actually be the result of bias in achievement tests that overestimates the talent of boys. This disparity between performance and test scores may be the result of deliberate camouflage of talents.

Nevertheless, there continues to be a gender gap favoring boys at the highest levels of achievement on standardized achievement tests. Of those students who

17

took the American College Testing (ACT) exams in 1988, 61% of students scoring above the 95th percentile on the composite score were male; 72% of students scoring in the 99th percentile on the composite score were male (Kerr & Colangelo, 1988). Males outperformed females at the highest levels on three of the four subtests of the ACT: mathematics, natural sciences, and social studies. There were 3 times as many males as females who earn perfect math scores; 5 times as many males earn perfect natural sciences scores; and 2 ½ times as many males get perfect social studies scores (Colangelo & Kerr, 1990). Only on the English subtest did females outperform males. Although the gap is narrowing, gifted males tend to hold the lead in math and science achievement test scores.

The lower composite scores for females on the ACT seem to be strongly related to the types of courses taken. Laing, Engen, and Maxey (1987) provided convincing evidence that much of the variance in ACT scores is accounted for by curriculum. Gifted adolescent females, at least until recently, take fewer and less challenging math, science, and social studies courses than gifted males.

In a study examining the relationship of self-efficacy to mathematical ability and achievement, Pajares (1996) reported that while gifted girls and gifted boys differed in their performance on math tasks, there was no difference in self-efficacy between the sexes. Their performance scores did not warrant greater self-efficacy for girls. Additionally, girls were less biased toward overconfidence in the ability to solve the math problems than boys – their self-beliefs more accurately reflected their ability. In light of the argument that some overestimation of ability may increase persistence and effort, this accuracy may be detrimental.

Adolescence brings changes in gifted girls' aspirations, expectations, attitudes, and achievement. Although the changes that occur for gifted girls today are subtler than those that occurred in the past, the theme of their lives is one of declining involvement with former achievement goals. By their sophomore year of college, many gifted women have changed their majors to less challenging disciplines; by their senior year they may have changed to lower career goals; and by five years after college graduation, they may have compromised their original dreams entirely (Kerr, 1997).

For gifted boys and young men, it is quite a different story. Career development tends to be linear for academically talented boys, with career aspirations, particularly in math and science, leading to academic majors and jobs in related areas. However, gifted boys also disengage from earlier goals by becoming less enthusiastic or even disillusioned about their career choices (Arnold & Denny, 1985). Unimaginative choices in vocational among gifted men often leads to a loss of interest in occupation and a quiet acceptance of an ordinary life (Kerr & Cohn, 2001).

Socialization - Gifted girls are more similar to gifted boys than to average girls in their interests, attitudes, and aspirations. Gifted girls apparently enjoy many play activities that have traditionally been associated with boys: outdoor activities, adventurous play, sports, and problem-solving activities. They also maintain feminine interests as well, such as playing with dolls and reading girls' magazines (Silverman, 1986; Terman & Oden, 1935). They are likely to be more open to playing with both children of both genders and often play with toys in a more complex way, inventing new games with even the most passive feminine toys (e.g., doing surgery upon a Barbie or marrying her off to Lego robot.)

Due to the dangerous nature of androgynous play interests for gifted boys within a homophobic society, they are usually restricted to boys' activities, despite the fact that many gifted boys are actually sensitive, nurturing, and caring (Pollack, 1999). Eminent women remember girlhoods full of exploration, adventure, and voracious reading. Although both eminent women and men spent a great deal of time in solitary activities as children, solitariness is not as strong a theme in eminent men's lives as it is in those of eminent women (Kerr, 1997).

Career Aspirations - Although sex-role-stereotyped career interests are well established by second grade in the general population of girls and boys, gifted girls may have career interests more similar to those of gifted boys (Silverman, 1986; Terman & Oden, 1935), and gifted girls tend to be less rigid in their sex role identification than average girls (Terman & Oden, 1935; Hay & Bakken, 1991; Kerr, 1997). Young gifted girls have high aspirations and vivid career fantasies: they dream of being paleontologists, astronauts, and ambassadors (Kerr, 1997). In the last twenty years, the aspirations of gifted girls have continued to climb, and their career goals are now just as high as those of gifted boys.

The major difference between the aspirations of gifted girls and gifted boys are the stronger altruistic and social motivations for girls, and stronger economic and achievement motivations for boys. Gifted girls, socialized to be caregivers, nearly always want careers that make people's lives better, or that make the world safer and more beautiful. Gifted boys, socialized still to be providers, are just as idealistic as girls, though they often choose careers that lead to higher salaries and status while fulfilling ideals.

Kelly (1992) has indicated that gifted adolescents do not have a higher career maturity than non-gifted students, suggesting that gifted children also require interventions that expose them to various career opportunities. He also indicated that gifted boys have a greater need for occupational information than gifted girls. Individual differences must be taken into consideration, however. For example, Hollinger (1991) stressed the need to provide highly individualistic career counseling for gifted adolescents that is sensitive to conflicting messages of multipotentiality and gender stereotypes that are acquired during this time of development.

Gifted adolescent girls' career aspirations appear to be changing. Whereas highly gifted girls, such as the top 1% of National Merit scholars, usually maintained high career aspirations in adolescence (Kaufmann, 1981), moderately gifted girls (those scoring in the upper 5% on IQ and achievement tests) tended to have declining career aspirations during adolescence (Kerr, 1983; 1985). Recently, however, gifted adolescent girls have been choosing college majors and career goals that have been considered nontraditional for women (Kerr & Colangelo, 1988). Among 12,330 girls scoring in the 95th percentile and above on the ACT, equal numbers of girls as boys chose majors in premedicine (17.0%). Social science (14.0%) and business (13.0%) were the most popular majors of this group. However, great disparities continue in one traditionally male career – engineering, where the proportions were 30.5% males to 7.9% females. When gifted adolescent girls were asked to name their career goals, they seemed to aim high. Although there are now equal numbers of gifted females interested in math, natural sciences, and health sciences as gifted males, gifted females continue to avoid the physical sciences, computer science, and engineering (Campbell & Clewell, 1999.)

Adjustment and Self-Esteem

In the moderately gifted range, gifted boys and girls are as healthy mentally as they are physically. While gifted children have higher social adjustment than average children, gifted girls tend to be better adjusted than gifted boys. Whether measured in terms of "social knowledge" (Terman & Oden, 1935), perceived self-competence (Chan, 1988) or absence of behavioral impairments on behavior ratings scales (Ludwig & Cullinan, 1984), gifted girls are remarkably free from childhood adjustment disorders. While the media has tended to emphasize the behavioral problems of gifted boys, there is no research evidence that gifted boys in general are at risk for psychological disorders. However, at the very highest levels of ability, both gifted boys and gifted girls may experience more adjustment problems. Terman and Oden (1935) and Hollingworth (1926) noted, fairly predictably, that children with the highest IQ, in general, suffered more adjustment problems, which may be as a result of their profoundly deviant intellectual abilities. In retrospective accounts of their lives, eminent women remember feeling "different" or "special" as children; even at a young age, it seems they were well aware of their deviance from the norm (Kerr, 1997).

Although girls in the late primary grades begin to fall somewhat behind the boys in achievement tests, they continue to surpass boys not only in grades, but also in overall adjustment and self-esteem. Both gifted boys and gifted girls before the age of 11 are strikingly confident.

They assert themselves in groups, and will argue for their opinions. They have high self-efficacy, believing they are good at many things, particularly schoolwork. At both five and eight years old, they have strong self-concepts; they have high opinions of their physical, academic, and social selves.

Evidence suggests that the majority of moderately gifted girls, like gifted boys, remain well-adjusted during adolescence (Janos & Robinson, 1985; Lessinger & Martinson, 1961; Terman & Oden, 1935). On personality inventories, gifted girls and boys are usually similar to or superior to average students on psychological characteristics associated with good mental health and adjustment. However, gifted adolescent girls may experience social anxiety and decreases in self-confidence. This was first shown in Groth and Holbert's (1969) cross-sectional study that showed an abrupt psychological shift at age 14 from wishes and needs related to achievement and self-esteem to wishes related to love and belonging. Her study showed that gifted younger girls tended to dream about success in school activities and accomplishments, while older gifted girls dreamed of popularity and intimate friendships. Kelly and Colangelo (1984) found that while gifted boys were superior to average boys in academic and social self-concepts, gifted girls were not similarly higher than average girls. Therefore, gifted boys seem to maintain their high self-esteem throughout the teen years, but gifted girls are not as fortunate.

In Kerr, Colangelo, and Gaeth's (1988) study of adolescents' attitudes toward their own giftedness, gifted girls were evidently quite concerned about the impact of their giftedness on attitudes of others. While they believed that there were some social advantages to being gifted, females saw more disadvantages than their male peers to being gifted. There was a deep ambivalence about the label *gifted*, as well as concern about negative images others might hold of that label.

Gifted boys' concern about giftedness is subtle (Kerr& Cohn, 2001). They strive to show that they are regular guys, despite their intelligence. Most gifted boys learn that it is acceptable for them to be gifted if they are also athletically competent, so they work to excel in the most popular sports. Those gifted adolescent boys who cannot shine on the playing fields may be labeled nerds and brains. In many cases, even these boys can develop a "machismo" based on their extraordinary technical ability, becoming admired by other students for their pyrotechnics on computers.

Issues of Special Concern to Gifted Girls
Socialization for Femininity

Self Esteem Plunge. There has been much controversy surrounding the findings of the AAUW study in 1991 that suggested that girls' self-esteem plunges between ages 11 and 17. (Kling, Hyde, Showers, & Buswell, 1999). Despite the critiques of the studies, it is clear that rates of eating disorders, substance abuse, and sexually transmitted diseases among teenage girls are on the increase. Although the majority of gifted girls continue to receive high grades and have very high levels of involvement in extracurricular activities, there is evidence that they are also vulnerable to loss of self-esteem (Lea-Wood & Clunies-Ross, 1995) and to risky behaviors that can jeopardize their goals and dreams (Kerr & Robinson Kurpius, 1999).

Studies of the self-concept of gifted girls show a similar decline to that of average girls. Terman's girls actually declined in their performance on the intelligence tests; administrators speculated that they were no longer trying as hard. Groth and Holbert's (1969) cross-sectional studies of gifted girls and women showed a sharp difference between the wishes of 10 and 14 year olds, with ten year olds valuing the pursuit of achievements and the enhancement of their self-esteem and fourteen year olds focusing almost entirely on desires for love and belonging. Fourteen year gifted girls seemed to believe that achievement and love were mutually exclusive. More recent studies have shown the same trend. Gifted girls' concept of themselves in all dimensions – physical, academic, and social – slides (Cseschlik & Rost, 1994).

The role of family, societal, and school expectations, achievement tests and grades, and girls' attitudes toward themselves have all been examined in an effort to understand what happens to adolescent gifted girls. Gifted girls, particularly in traditional families and cultures, are expected to do an "about–face" in adolescence (Kerr, 1997; Reis, Callahan, & Goldsmith, 1996); there is strong evidence that women who become eminent or achieving in Hispanic and Asian cultures are those who receive family encouragement that is out of the ordinary (Kitano,1996; 1997; 1998). Though intelligence in pre-adolescent girls is considered a positive characteristic, with little girls being encouraged in their schoolwork and precocious behavior, adolescence brings a new expectation - gifted girls should turn their attention to becoming an attractive potential mate. Few cultures perceive intelligence as an attractive characteristic in a woman; men tend to marry their equals or inferiors in ability (Kerr, 1997). As a result, most bright girls adjust to their culture's expectations of them. Girls emulate the media portrayals of women. Gifted girls may focus their intelligence and creativity on diet schemes, shopping, and grooming rituals. In addition, gifted girls may become social experts, working their peer group in such as way as to increase their status and popularity with Machiavellian skill.

Adolescent gifted girls enter counseling for a wide variety of reasons, although again, it must be stressed that the incidence of severe behavioral problems is much lower in gifted girls than in average girls (Janos & Robinson, 1985). At-risk behaviors include bulimia and anorexia, drug and alcohol abuse, and unsafe sex and unwanted pregnancy. In gifted girls, these behaviors take on different meanings than with the general population of girls (Kerr & Robinson Kurpius, 1999). Eating disorders are often an extension of adolescent gifted girls' high needs for achievement. When society demands a thin, attractive body as opposed to an educated mind, these girls may attempt to become the thinnest girls in the school. Drug and alcohol abuse are compounded by gifted girls' ability to hide their problem behaviors, to create cover stories, and to distract adults with academic achievement. Even alcohol abuse can be sort of achievement for the gifted girl who wants to prove her ability to binge with the boys. On the other hand, unsafe sex and unwanted pregnancies are sometimes the result of gifted girls wanting to prove their femininity; early sexual activity may mean acceptance into the social group by a girl who is otherwise an outsider.

Inequity in the Classroom

Portrayals of girls and women in academic materials are little improvement on media portrayals. Zittelman and Sadker (2003) and Sadker and Sadker (1994) analyzed the content of commonly used math, language arts, and history books and found that girls and women were greatly under represented. The items on tests and achievement tests, particularly in science and math, feature problems that are more interesting to boys than to girls, such as items about machines, wagering (e.g., If you had a poker hand that had two aces...), and sports. Girls do less well on these items, but perform better on items with the same level of difficulty that pertain to issues of interest to them: nature and animals, arts and crafts, and people.

Adolescent gifted girls may also be at a disadvantage in the classroom due to teacher attitudes. Siegle and Reis (1998) found that teachers perceive their gifted girls as working harder and producing higher quality work than gifted boys, but still assign higher grades to the boys. Girls appear to accept their teachers' judgments, and then evaluate themselves as less able than the boys in mathematics and science. Cooley, Chauvin, and Karnes (1984) found similar stereotyping, with teachers perceiving gifted boys as having superior critical thinking skills and problem solving abilities, and perceiving gifted girls as having superior creative writing abilities. Although most teachers are opposed to sex role stereotyping attempt to avoid stereotyping in general, they still tend to see gifted boys as liking math and being better at it than girls (Fennema, Carpenter, Franke, Levi et al., 1996).

Potential sources of bias need to be removed from the program of study as well as the identification procedures. Ample evidence exists of inequitable instruction in the classroom (Sadker & Sadker, 1985). Boys receive more attention from teachers than girls throughout their education; boys are called on more often and are more frequently rewarded for calling out answers, while girls are reprimanded for the same response. Boys also receive more informative responses from teachers; Sadker and Sadker found that girls receive more "accepting" responses from teachers, whereas boys receive more praise and criticism. Boys receive more instructional attention, receiving detailed instructions on the correct approach to tasks, while girls frequently are simply given the right answers. These differential teacher responses do not seem to be the result of deliberate discrimination, but rather a response to differing behaviors between boys and girls and unconscious socialized attitudes. Similar studies have not been done specifically with gifted children or in the context of a gifted education program. Nevertheless, there are some indicators that gifted girls suffer from differential treatment.

Although the causes of teachers' differential treatment of girls and boys may run deep, the remedy may not be difficult or complex. Sadker and Sadker (1984) found that most teachers wanted to teach in a nonsexist manner and were eager to learn how. Brief training workshops were effective in improving equitable behavior; teachers can learn to call on girls as often as they call on boys, to give girls informative responses, praising and criticizing in detail, to reward girls' assertiveness in the classroom, and to resist "over helping" girls by giving them answers or solving problems for them.

Another perspective on equity in the classroom instruction is given by Licht and Dweck (1984), who showed that girls learn to attribute the causes of their successes and failures differently than boys. Possibly because of bland teacher responses and over helping, girls learn to attribute their successes to luck and effort and their failures to lack of ability. This may lead them to avoid coursework that they believe requires considerable effort and for which they believe they lack the ability (Eccles, 1987). Therefore, girls need to be taught to have confidence in their abilities and to believe that their efforts are effective.

Gifted girls must be given specific information about their superior abilities very early (Kerr, 1985). They should be helped to understand their intellectual strength and to see how their abilities can help them in their class work. Gifted girls need to perceive their giftedness not as a mysterious force out of their control, but rather a set of potentials that, when combined with effort, can lead to extraordinary accomplishment.

Changing teacher behavior is only one aspect of removing bias from the education of gifted girls. Boy-centered textbooks, literature, and activities may discourage bright girls from pursuing interest even in those areas in which they excel and which they enjoy. This can be particularly a problem in science and math classes, where experimenters, teachers, and the subject of study are rarely female or feminine. These materials should be checked for balance of presentation. Do illustrative pictures have an equal number of males and females? Are female authors represented? Are the roles of women in history and current events represented? Further, the American Association of University of Women (1992) also suggests that schools and communities should encourage the study of math and science by girls by providing role models in science and technological fields that are women.

Gifted girls' tendency to be able to read popular adult literature while still very young may occasionally have negative effects; popular novels and magazines are often much more sexist than school materials or age-appropriate materials. While the restriction of the amount or type of reading engaged in by gifted girls is not encouraged, teachers and librarians should discuss with bright girls the gender stereotypes that are inherent in many recreational reading materials. "Innoculating" bright girls against negative portrayals of women with biographies of eminent women and stories about strong, active, courageous girls may be the best approach to combating sexism in print (Kerr, 1985).

According to the research of Holland and Eisenhart (1991), as well as research on high school valedictorians by Arnold (1993), a culture of romance which is virulently inimical to female achievement still thrives in coeducational colleges and universities. By the time a gifted young woman has graduated from college, she is likely to have lowered her estimate of her own intelligence, changed to a less challenging major, and lowered her career aspirations. She is much more likely than her gifted male peers to have abandoned her math and science interests, and is less likely to pursue graduate training in these fields. After college, she is more likely to follow her boyfriend or husband to his job than to have him follow her. She is the one most likely to have major childrearing responsibilities. And although it is now the norm for gifted women to combine work and family, gifted women continue to be more likely than gifted men to give up full-time for part-time work and to give up leadership positions (Kerr, 1997.)

Although the gifted male in college has not given up his math and science interests, he is in danger of giving up something much more important: his opportunity to choose a career based on his most deeply held values. Most gifted men will give up their interests in creative arts, languages, humanities and literature because they do not seem lucrative, or perhaps manly, enough (Colangelo & Kerr, 1990). The majority of gifted men choose college majors from among the same four areas: engineering, pre-med, pre-law, and business. The unimaginative majors of gifted men often lead to dissatisfaction in adulthood, with little hope of changing careers due to the enormous investment of time and money that goes into higher status occupations. Gifted men may end up overworked and unavailable to family as they pursue what they have been socialized to pursue: status, power, and riches.

By the time gifted males and females have reached adulthood, the development of their talent has been influenced by gender socialization. For different reasons, they have often compromised away the promise of their giftedness. Except for those boys and girls who have the courage and support to challenge gender roles, most gifted boys and girls do succumb to society's image of what achievement constitutes.

A telling example comes from our recent study of gifted students' perfect future day fantasies: their favorite vision of what they might be doing in ten years. For twenty years, I have been sitting behind the one-way mirror observing groups of students as they discuss their dreams and goals with their counselors and each other. My favorite technique for assessing students' expectations about their own future is a visualization exercise called "The Perfect Future Day Fantasy." In this fantasy, students imagine a day from morning to midnight, ten years in their own future. They are asked to imagine where they are living, what they are wearing, with whom they are living, and what kind of work they are doing. A typical college male's fantasy goes something like this: "I wake up and get in my car, a really nice rebuilt '67 Mustang, and then I go to work. I think I'm some kind of a manager of a computer firm, and then I go home. When I get there, my wife is there at the door (she has a really nice figure), she has a drink for me, and she's made a great meal. We watch TV or maybe play with the kids." Here is the typical college female's fantasy: "I wake up and my husband and I get in our twin Jettas, and I go to the law firm where I work. Then after work, I go home and he's pulling up in the driveway at the same time. We go in and have a glass of wine and we make an omelet together and eat by candlelight. Then the nanny brings the children in and we play with them till bedtime." What's wrong with this picture?

Women dream of dual career bliss, while men dream that they might find a woman who wants to stay home and take care of them and the children. Despite extraordinary changes in the career expectations of women, many college men have yet to acknowledge the changes in gender roles that women's expectations imply. In an interesting case of whether the glass is 70% full or 30% empty, Astin (1998) showed how the percentage of men who endorse the item, "The activities of married women are best confined to the home and family," dropped from 66.5% to 30.8% over 25 years. The percentage of women who endorsed this item changed from 44.3% in 1966 to 19% in 1996. Although the researchers praise this drop, the fact remains that 3 out of 10 men that a college woman might meet may expect that after marriage she will "confine" herself to caring for him and his children. It is also likely that men who publicly endorse equitable relationships secretly wish for a more traditional lifestyle. Conversely, college women have romantic, yet egalitarian relationships as their goals, for which they have no roadmaps. Therefore, in both work and relationships, gifted men and women may sabotage their own dreams to fit into the gender roles that have been prescribed for them.

As educators and counselors, we can prevent these compromised dreams by helping both girls and boys to discover their own meaning of femininity and masculinity, and by helping both girls and boys to make choices based on their most deeply held values. A workshop called Values based Career Counseling helps both adolescents and college-age students to make decisions in this way (Kerr & Erb, 1991); the workshops created by Kerr and Robertson Kurpius (1999) for talented at risk adolescent girls are based on this model.

It is important, however, to reach children earlier in life. Teachers and parents can help their children to discover the work values that will give meaning to their lives. Both girls and boys can be encouraged to be achieving in order to accomplish their own goals, rather than to accomplish the goals of others. Girls need to continue to be encouraged to lead, but boys also need to be taught that there is no shame in following a girl leader. Both gifted girls and boys need relationship education, for bright women and men will need to learn to love and work together in the future. Girls and boys can be taught to respect one another's goals through the modeling of their teachers and parents.

Conclusion

Much as been learned since Lewis Terman and Melita Oden first described the gifted girl, but much remains to be learned. As programs spread for the encouragement of gifted girls, it is important that research continue on the ways of identifying giftedness in girls, guiding their talent development, and providing them with mentoring, challenging education, and career opportunities.

References:

American Association of University Women (1992). *The AAUW Report: How schools shortchange girls, executive report.* Washington, D.C.: AAUW Education Foundation.

Astin, A.W. (1998). The changing American college student: Thirty year trends. *Review of Higher Education,* 21, 2, 115-35.

Arnold, K. D. (1993). Academically talented women in the 1980's: the Illinois Valedictorian Project. In K. D. Hulbert & D. L. Schuster (Eds.), *Women's lives through time: Educated American women of the twentieth century.* (pp.393-414). San Francisco: Jossey-Bass.

Arnold, K., & Denny, T. (1985, April). *The lives of academic achievers: The career aspirations of male and female high school valedictorians and salutatorians.* Paper presented at the annual meeting of the American Educational Research Association, Chicago, Illinois.

Campbell, P., & Clewell, B. C. (1999). Science, math and girls: Still a long way to go. *Education Week,* 9/15/99, 50-51.

Chan, L. K. S. (1988). The perceived competence of intellectually talented students. *Gifted Child Quarterly, 32,* 310-315.

Colangelo, N., & Kerr, B. A. (1990). Extreme academic talent: Profiles of perfect scorers. *Journal of Educational Psychology, 82,* 404-409.

Cooley, D., Chauvin, J. C., & Karnes, F. A. (1984). Gifted females: A comparison of attitudes by male and female teachers. *Roeper Review, 6,* 164-167.

Czeschlik, T. & Rost, D. H. (1994). Socio-emotional adjustment in elementary school boys and school girls: Does giftedness make a difference? *Roeper Vewier, 16,* 294-297.

Fennema, E., Carpenter, T. P., Franke, M. L., & Levi, L. et al. (1996). A longitudinal study of learning to use children's thinking in mathematics instruction. *Journal for Research in Mathematics Education, 27,* 403-434.

Firestone, Shulamith (1970). *The dialectics of sex: The case for feminist revolution.* New York: Morrow.

Gallagher, J. J. (1985). *Teaching the gifted child* (3rd ed.). Boston: Allyn and Bacon.

Groth, N. J., & Holbert, P. (1969). Hierarchical needs of gifted boys and girls in the affective domain. *Gifted Child Quarterly, 13,* 129-133.

Hay, C. A., & Bakken, L. (1991). Gifted sixth-grade girls: Similarities and differences in attitudes among gifted girls, non-gifted peers, and their mothers. *Roeper Review, 13,* 158-160.

Holland, D. C., & Eisenhart, M. A. (1990). *Educated in romance: Women, achievement, and college culture.* Chicago: University of Chicago Press.

Hollinger, C. L. (1991). Facilitating the career development of gifted young women. *Roeper Review, 13,* 135-139.

Hollingworth, L.S. (1926). *Gifted children: Their nature and nurture.* New York: Macmillan.

Janos, P. M., & Robinson, N. M. (1985). Psychosocial development in intellectually gifted children. In M. O'Brien, & F. D. Horowitz (Eds.), *The gifted and talented: Developmental perspectives.* (pp.149-195). Washington, DC, US: American Psychological Association.

Kauffman, F. (1981). The 1964-1968 Presidential Scholars: A follow-up study. *Exceptional Children, 48,* 2.

Kelly, K. (1992). Career maturity of young gifted adolescents: A replication study. *Journal for the education of the gifted, 16,* 36-45.

Kerr, B. A. (1983). Raising the career aspirations of gifted girls. *Vocational Guidance Quarterly, 32*, 37-44.

Kerr, B. A. (1985). *Smart girls, gifted women.* Columbus: Ohio Psychology.

Kerr, B. A. (1997). *Smart Girls: A new psychology of girls, women, and giftedness.* Scottsdale, AZ: Gifted Psychology Press.

Kerr, B. A., & Cohn, S. J. (2001). *Smart boys: Talent, manhood, and the search for meaning.* Scottsdale, AZ: Great Potential Press.

Kerr, B. A., & Colangelo, N. (1988). The college plans of academically talented students. *Journal of Counseling and Development, 67,* 42-49.

Kerr, B. A., Colangelo, N., & Gaeth, J. (1988). Gifted adolescents' attitudes toward their giftedness. *Gifted Child Quarterly, 32,* 245-247.

Kerr, B. A., & Erb, C. (1991). Career counseling with academically talented students: Effects of a value-based intervention. *Journal of Counseling Psychology, 38,* 309-341.

Kerr, B. A., & Robinson Kurpius, S. E. (1999). Brynhilde's Fire: Talent, risk and betrayal in the lives of gifted girls. In J. LeRoux (Ed.), *Connecting the gifted community worldwide* (261-271). Ottawa: World Council on Gifted and Talented.

Kitano, M. K. & Perkins, C. O. (1996). International gifted women: Developing a critical resource. *Roeper Review, 19,* 1, 34-40.

Kitano, M. K.(1997). Gifted Asian American women. *Journal for the Education of the Gifted, 21,* 1, 3-37.

Kitano, M. K. (1998). Gifted Latina women. *Journal for the Education of the Gifted, 21,* 2, 131-159.

Kling, K. C., Hyde, J. S., Showers, C., & Buswell, B. (1999). Gender differences in self-esteem: A meta-analysis. *Psychological Bulletin,* 125, 470-500

Laing, J., Engen, H. B., & Maxey, J. (1987). Relationships between ACT scores and high school courses. *ACT Research Reports,* Jan. 1987, Tech-Rpt 87-3.

Lea-Wood, S. S., & Clunies-Ross, Graham. (1995). Self-esteem of gifted adolescent girls in Austrailian schools. *Roeper Review, 17,* 195-197.

Leroux, J.A. (1994). A tapestry of values: Gifted women speak out. *Gifted Education International, 9,* 167-171.

Lessinger, L. M., & Martinson, R. A. (1961). The use of the California Psychological Inventory with gifted pupils. *Personnel and Guidance Journal, 39,* 572-575.

Licht, B. G., & Dweck, C. S. (1984). Determinants of academic achievement: The interaction of children's achievement orientations with skill area. *Developmental Psychology, 20,* 628-636.

Ludwig, G., & Cullinan, D. (1984). Behavior problems of gifted and nongifted elementary school girls and boys. *Gifted Child Quarterly, 28,* 37-40.

National Institute of Mental Health (1993). *Eating Disorders.* NIH Publication No. 93-3477/ Washington D. C.: US Department of Health and Human Services.

National Council for Educational Statistics. (2004). The nation's report card: National assessment of educational progress. Web site available at http://nces.ed.gov/pubsearch/ getpubcats.asp?sid=031

Pajares, F. (1996). Self-efficacy beliefs and mathematical problem-solving of gifted students. *Contemporary educational psychology, 21,* 325-344.

Phillips, L. (1998). *The girls report.* New York, NY: National Council for Research on Women.

Pollack, W. (1999). *Real boys: Rescuing our sons from the myths of boyhood.* Owl Publishing Company.

Reis, S. M. (1995). Talent ignored, talent diverted: The cultural context underlying giftedness in females. *Gifted Child Quarterly, 39,* 162-170.

Reis, S. M., Callahan, C. M., & Goldsmith, D. (1996). Attitudes of adolescent gifted girls and boys toward education, achievement, and the future. In K. D. Noble, & K. D. Arnold (Eds.), *Remarkable women: Perspectives on female talent development.* (pp.209-224). Cresskill, NJ: Hampton Press, Inc.

Sadker, M. & Sadker, D. (1985). *Interventions that promote equity and effectiveness in student-teacher interaction.* Paper presented at the annual meeting of the American Educational Research Association, Chicago, Illinois.

Sadker, M. & Sadker, D. (1994). *Failing at fairness: How America's schools cheat girls.* New York: Charles Scribner's Sons.

Siegle, D., & Reis, S. M. (1998). Gender differences in teacher and student perceptions of gifted students' ability and effort. *Gifted Children Quarterly, 42,* 39-47.

Silverman, L. K. (1986). What happens to the gifted girl? In Maker, C. J. (Ed.), *Critical issues in gifted education: Defensible programs for the gifted* (pp. 43-89). Rockville, MD: Aspen.

Terman, L. M., & Oden, M. H. (1935). *Genetic studies of genius: Vol. 3. The promise of youth.* Stanford, CA: Stanford University Press.

Tomlinson-Keasey, C.(1999). Gifted women's lives. In N. Colangelo, & S. G. Assouline (Eds.), *Talent development.* Scottsdale, AZ: Gifted Psychology Press.

Zittleman, K.& Sadker, D. (2003). The unfinished gender revolution. *Educational Leadership,* 60, 4, 59-63.

2

Talent and Risk in College: The Problem of Persistence

Sarah E. Lowery
Sharon E. Robinson Kurpius
Barbara Kerr

A woman talented in the areas of science, technology, engineering, or math (STEM) may enter college with a confusing mixture of qualities. Her career goals are likely to be higher than that of an average woman and as high in status as that of a gifted man (Kerr, 1997). She probably has higher grades than similarly gifted young men, but she may be less prepared for the academic challenges that await her (Phillips, 1998). Despite her strong abilities in mathematics and science, her course work may have been less rigorous.

Several studies have shown that the majority of women begin college without adequate exposure to and encouragement regarding the sciences (Hartman, 1995). Additionally, incoming freshman women often exhibit a deficiency in the basic science and mathematics knowledge needed to persist in STEM majors (Chang, 2002). Furthermore, Chang suggested that many female undergraduates believe that the technical nature of STEM fields is not representative of life skills of creative thinking and communication. Similarly, Seymour (1992) stated that the image that scientific careers hold often does not appeal to young women's desires to help others and to have a family. These obstacles may be accompanied by a fear of low achievement and subsequently an avoidance of science courses and majors altogether (Hartman, 1995).

The academically talented young woman may begin college with high educational and career aspirations and may even expect to do post-graduate studies. However, her self-esteem, which has been declining since early adolescence, is now at the lowest point ever (AAUW, 1991). The talented young woman may have lost confidence in her own voice, finding it difficult to express her own opinions and, therefore, choosing peer acceptance over individuality. She may have trouble asserting herself in class and may not respond well to criticism (Brown & Gilligan, 1992). When a young, talented college woman receives her first "C" in a freshman math or science class, she often decides that she lacks the ability to perform in math and science (Dweck, 1995; Kerr, 1995). The shock and disappointment she has after receiving such a "horrible" grade may cause her to rethink and even change her major from that of science or math to something "easier" so she may avoid those negative feelings. For these young women, perceptions of competition and difficulty with majoring in the sciences may be paired with low self-ratings of ability in traditionally male-dominated analytical fields (Chang, 2002). Furthermore, Seymour and Hewitt (1997) reported that cases of math anxiety and instructors' lowered expectations for women have also been shown to dissuade women from participating in STEM majors.

Academic Persistence

Research has suggested that both academic and psychosocial factors are associated with college persistence and attrition (Terenzini & Pascarella, 1997). Academic persistence has been widely studied and has been found to be related to many variables including self-concept, self-perception of intellectual ability, instructor support (Boutler, 2002), educational self-efficacy (Gloria & Robinson Kurpius, 2001; Lent, Brown, & Larkin, 1986; Zimmerman, Bandura, & Martinez-Pons, 1992), choice of major (Leppel, 2001), stress (Pancer, Hunsberger, Pratt, & Alisat, 2000), university environment (Bennett & Okinaka, 1990; Gloria, Robinson Kurpius, Hamilton, & Willson, 1999), and academic ability (Daugherty & Lane, 1999; Johnson, 1994). According to data files from the American College Testing Program (ACT), rates of institutional attrition across the United States have remained fairly stable since 1983. Of the approximately 2.8 million students who enroll in higher education for the first time, over 1.6 million leave the first college they attended prior to graduation. Of these students, approximately 1.2 million (42.8%) will leave higher education without earning a degree (Boutler, 2002).

Gender Discrepancy and STEM.

Persistence not only pertains to attrition rates from college but also to attrition rates from college majors (Leppel, 2001). Despite significant increases in enrollment for women in law, medicine, and business (Campbell & Clewell, 1999), women are still drastically underrepresented in the physical sciences, engineering, and technology programs (e.g., Betz, 1994; Chang, 2002; Eccles, 1987). In 1995, 118,000 men as compared to only 64,000 women graduated with degrees in these areas (Hill, 1997). The National Science Board (NSB, 2002) reported that in 1998 women comprised only 37% of the science, math, and engineering bachelor's degrees received while they received 56% of the bachelor's degrees granted overall.

For engineering degrees, the numbers are even lower. The National Science Foundation (NSF; 2000) reported that in 1997, women accounted for 19% of the total undergraduate enrollment in engineering, up from 15 percent in 1987. According to Beder (1999), Americans typically define engineers as being male, socially inept, and unfashionable. She believes that the poor image associated with engineering may affect high school students' career decisions and subsequently leads to a shortage of female engineers. In an examination of teachers' understanding of Design Engineering Technology (DET), Robinson Kurpius, Krause, Yasar, Roberts, and Baker (2004) studied 98 ethnically diverse teachers (56 women and 42 men) representing 27 school districts in Arizona. Their findings indicated that teachers held more negative stereotypes regarding the ability of women and racial/ethnic minorities do to well in DET than they did for boys or students in general. Moreover, teacher perceptions of minority students' abilities were significantly more positive than were their perceptions of female students. According to the National Science Board (2002) underrepresented minorities (e.g., African-Americans, Latinos, and Native Americans) received just 12 percent of STEM degrees conferred in 2002. Despite many efforts at both local and national levels to increase the number of women and minorities enrolled and retained in STEM majors, women and ethnic/racial minorities are still drastically underrepresented as compared to men.

The answer to the question of why the number of women, regardless of race/ethnicity, in STEM majors is so significantly less than the number of men still remains unknown. However, there are many factors that may contribute to women's lack of parallel achievement in the STEM majors. Ware and Lee (1988) studied choice of majors for male and female students. They found that women who place a high emphasis on their personal lives and future family plans were less likely than other women to major in science. For male students, the importance of having a family seemed to have no significant influence on choice of major. Orenstein (1994) suggested that young women often link academic accomplishment with denial of pleasure. For example, to be fully academically successful, a young woman must not date at all, not have children, and live a lonely life. This type of thinking is dangerous, because it is likely that women will fall in love before their educational goals are attained (Orenstein). If these young women feel that they must relinquish their educational goals in order to satisfy their "pleasure" needs, it is likely that they will never achieve their dreams or maybe never even get in touch with what dreams they are "allowed" to have.

Positive role models may also have an influence on women's pursuit of STEM careers. Hackett, Esposito, and O'Halloran (1989) studied the impact of the perceived influence of female and male role models, gender role attitudes, and performance self-esteem on women's career salience and career-related aspirations and choices in 107 senior college women. The researchers found mothers' influence as a role model to be positively related to the choice of a nontraditional (e.g., math, science) college major for young women. Additionally, positive influence of female teachers was found to be predictive of career salience and educational aspirations. Thus, for women interested in STEM majors and careers, the presence of positive female role models may represent an integral aspect of persistence in these arenas.

A 1999 study by Turner and Bowen indicated that changes in Scholastic Aptitude Test (SAT) scores have not been able to explain sufficiently gender differences in choice of college majors. They suggested that the discrepancies may be attributed to differences in career preferences, labor market expectations, and college experiences. Leppel (2001) suggested that men and women in nontraditional majors may feel "more negative pressure or less positive emotional support from friends and family than students in other majors. Therefore, the current cost of continuing in that major may be increased. Some students in nontraditional majors may decide to change to more traditional majors. Thus, students in nontraditional majors may have lower persistence rates" (p. 330).

The constraints on women's persistence and achievement in STEM careers and majors are complex. Women interested in mathematics and science face a number of barriers that may impact their career goals and dreams. It seems that positive role models, perceptions of intellectual ability, social support, and perceptions of the university environment represent some of the factors that may serve as a prophylactic against women prematurely dropping out of STEM majors.

Risk Factors

One reason young women may have difficulty persisting in STEM majors may be the "at-risk" status they carry from adolescence into their college years. Factors including substance abuse, sexual risk taking, and suicide may have harmful effects on the present lives and futures of young women. These and other negative behaviors place young women at risk for denying themselves the chance to achieve their aspirations.

In general, adolescent girls have endured a long history of being ignored by psychologists, researchers, and academicians. Until recently, academics failed to study them and therapists had no theoretically-based treatments for young women (Pipher, 1994). In 1992, the American Association of University Women (AAUW) and the Wellesley Center for Research on Women published a study entitled "How Schools Shortchange Girls." Prior to this pivotal work and the subsequent media attention it received, few outside academia were aware of the decline in female academic performance and drive. The general public was oblivious to the fact that female students had been steadily lowering their expectations with regard to their own performance and had ignored many challenges and opportunities that could enhance their scholastic growth (Sebrechts, 1999).

In recent years, researchers have become increasingly concerned about adolescents who are considered "at-risk." In addition, mainstream, academic, and political minds have all worried about various threats to girls including waning self-esteem, eating disorders, and promiscuous sexual activity (Kenny, 2000). Within the "at-risk" label, behavioral scientists study the effects of variables that may include gender, race, class, and ethnicity. For example, substance abuse among females can be particularly concerning because of the continued rise in this risky behavior as well as the consequences associated with it (Gagliardi, Robinson Kurpius, Gloria, & Lambert, 2004). Abuse of alcohol and drugs within this population increases the probability of risky sexual behaviors associated with pregnancy, sexually transmitted diseases, and forced sexual situations (Beauvais, 1992; Harper & Robinson, 1999).

The extreme pressure adolescent girls often experience to fit into a culturally defined norm may also place them at risk for pursuing hazardous behaviors that may negatively impact their futures. In her widely popular book, *Reviving Ophelia*, Mary Pipher (1994) examined the psyches of adolescent girls. She remarked on Alice Miller's (1981) *The Drama of the Gifted Child* (1981) in which Miller noted that some of her patients lost their "true selves" in early childhood. They could be authentic or they could be loved. If they chose authenticity, they were abandoned by their parents. If they chose love, they abandoned their true selves. Parents, because of influences in their own childhoods, regarded aspects of their children's personalities as unacceptable. Children sensed this and stopped expressing unacceptable feelings and engaging in unacceptable behaviors. As the child disowned the true self, the false self was elevated. If the false self was validated from the outside world, the person was temporarily happy.

Pipher (1994) related Miller's work to girls suggesting that the American culture, rather than parental influence, is responsible for splitting adolescent girls into true and false selves. She suggested that during adolescence, girls experience social pressure to put aside their authentic selves and, therefore, display only a portion of their talents. Adolescent girls become especially vulnerable to losing their authentic selves due to their developmental level (e.g., effects of puberty), American culture, and societal pressure to distance oneself from parents. First, adolescence is a time when girls experience extreme changes in their bodies and minds including outward physical changes combined with inward hormonal changes. Second, although the American culture outwardly promotes the abolishment of inequities, sexism, lookism, and racism are still rampant and may be particularly harmful to young women. Pipher wrote, "the lip service paid to equality makes the reality of discrimination even more confusing" (p.121). The culturally mixed messages experienced by girls and women lead to confusion and ambivalence over how one should behave. Third, American girls are expected to distance themselves from their parents becoming "independent" during this time of confusion. Just when adolescent girls need the most support to sort out feelings of ambivalence, they are encouraged by the surrounding culture to break free of parental constraints. As teenagers, females may also be starting to become aware of the many ways that society expects them to behave. For example, they are inundated with images of ideal women (e.g., excessively slim) and must consciously or unconsciously struggle to understand the meanings of these constraining images. While grappling with these important and complex issues, the young women are most likely experiencing pressures from their peers and a natural desire to be independent and assert themselves with parents. Phillips (1998) suggested that as young women become more assertive, they often assume problems that have traditionally been associated with young men such as substance abuse, violence, and self-destructiveness. Thus, as young women distance themselves from their parents at younger ages, they become more vulnerable to risky behaviors that may deter their goals and dreams.

A young woman's peers may also strongly influence her thoughts and behaviors and place her at risk of losing sight of her ambitions. Research has shown that peers influence adolescents' decisions around behavioral choices such as clothing, activities, and friendships (Kandel, 1985). Additionally, numerous studies have highlighted the importance of peers' behaviors and attitudes regarding deviance such as cigarette smoking, drug use, and sexual activity (Benda & DiBlasio, 1994; Hart, 2000; Whitback, Conger, Simons, & Kao, 1993).

According to Kerr (1997) peer relationships may be even more important to gifted youth because of their strong needs for love and belonging. Since peer relationships strongly influence risky behaviors, high-ability adolescents may be particularly at risk when they associate with others engaging in negative behavior. Kerr and Robinson Kurpius (1999) suggested that in gifted girls, at-risk behaviors may assume different meanings than when related to girls of the general population. For example, body image issues, which often subsequently result in eating disordered behaviors, may serve as an extension of the perfectionism and high needs for achievement that adolescent gifted girls often crave (Kerr & Foley-Nicpon, 2003). Robinson Kurpius and Kerr (2001) suggested that young, talented women may even try to be the "best" at various at-risk behaviors. They may attempt to become the thinnest girls in the school as an answer to society's demands for an attractive body over an educated mind. Gifted young women's abilities to hide their problem behaviors through academic achievement and cover stories may exacerbate and prolong issues with drugs and alcohol. Furthermore, early sexual activity, unsafe sex, and unwanted pregnancies may sometimes be the result of gifted girls' attempts at proving their femininity (Robinson Kurpius & Kerr).

Young women interested in STEM majors and careers face many social, cultural, and environmental obstacles to the achievement of their goals. Developmental changes brought on by puberty, institutional sexism, detachment from parents, negative peer influence, and risky behaviors may compound the already uphill battle young women must face when pursing STEM careers and majors. In order for talented young women to achieve their potentials in mathematics and science, particular attention must be paid to the unique ways in which they may be affected by these barriers.

Self Beliefs

Self beliefs refer to how people understand themselves in relationship to the environment. Two types of self-beliefs that have been found to be related to academic persistence are self-esteem and educational self-efficacy (Gloria & Robinson Kurpius, 2001).

Self-Esteem. For over 40 years, the concept of self-esteem has occupied an important space in psychology (Rosenberg, Schooler, Schoenbach, & Rosenberg, 1995). Theories related to self-esteem or self-concept have been widely studied with a more recent, expanding focus on self-esteem in young women. Self-esteem, also referred to as self-concept, has been called the "totality of the individual's thoughts and feelings with reference to the self as an object" (Rosenberg, 1986, p. 103). Jourard (1974) stated that a person's self concept comprises all of his or her beliefs about his or her own nature. This includes strengths, weaknesses, growth possibilities, and behavior patterns and experiences. Zimbardo (1979) reported that self-esteem developed from feedback about one's worth and competence.

In the midst of societal pressure regarding how women should behave, adolescent women struggle with self-esteem issues that permeate many aspects of their lives. The existence of a self-esteem plunge in girls between the ages of 11 and 17 is widely acknowledged (Kerr & Foley Nicpon, 2003; Lea-Wood & Clunies-Ross, 1995). This decline in self-esteem seems to be carried into college and impacts the way in which young women perceive themselves both socially and academically.

Many believe that intelligence may protect gifted young women from threats to their self-esteem (Kerr & Foley Nicpon, 2003). However, despite excellent performance in the classroom, gifted girls often develop internal barriers that stop them from realizing their potential (Robinson Kurpius & Kerr, 2001). Additionally, researchers have found that students' self-esteem and educational self-efficacy are positively related to persistence in school (Gloria et al., 1999; Robinson Kurpius, Chee, Rayle, & Arredondo, 2003).

The connection between self-esteem and career decision-making has long been studied (Hull Blanks, Robinson Kurpius, Befort, Sollenberger, Foley Nicpon, & Huser, 2004). As early as 1953, Super argued that one's self perception was central to one's process of choosing a vocation. Super and Bohn (1971), found that vocational choice was actually a "translation" of one's self. They argued that self-opinions are in fact highly related to career selection and goal-setting. More recently, Hollinger and Fleming (1984) found that low self-esteem in adolescent women often serves as an obstacle to achieving their career potential. In addition to self-esteem, educational self-efficacy has been an important variable in understanding young women's academic persistence, especially in STEM-related fields.

Educational Self-Efficacy.

Bandura (1989) described self-efficacy as one's belief in one's abilities to accomplish specific tasks. Self-efficacy also includes, "self-perceptions of one's efficacy influences, one's thought patterns, actions, and emotions. The stronger the 'perceived self-efficacy,' the higher the goals people set for themselves and the firmer their commitment to them" (Bandura 1982; p. 1175).

Researchers have argued that self-efficacy influences the career development of women. Hacket and Betz (1981) extended Bandura's (1977) self-efficacy theory to include vocational behavior. In their theoretical work, they posited that the formulation of women's career goals strongly relates to self-efficacy and may be especially useful in understanding women's career development. For example, they hypothesized that self-efficacy beliefs are related to people's range of perceived career options and persistence and success in their chosen fields. A clear understanding of the relationship between self-efficacy and career goals may be especially useful for women interested in STEM careers. For instance, a young woman with high self-efficacy beliefs related to math and science may then have an increased range of perceived career options including non-traditional STEM careers.

Gender and ethnicity have also been shown to impact self-beliefs and self-efficacy. Luzzo and McWhirter (2001) suggested that career and vocational psychologists must consider gender and ethnic differences in the perception of educational and career-related barriers to success. They studied perceived career-related barriers in 168 female and 118 male undergraduate students and found that women and ethnic minorities anticipated significantly more career-related barriers than did men and European American students. In a study of 530 female undergraduates, Rayle, Arredondo, and Robinson Kurpius (2004, in press) found that personal and family valuing of education and self-esteem were positively related to educational self-efficacy. Lent et al. (1986) highlighted the importance of exploring self-efficacy beliefs in addition to interests, values, and abilities when helping students with career planning. The researchers assessed 105 undergraduates (75 men and 30 women) participating in a career planning course on science and engineering on measures of self-efficacy and educational/vocational indecision. Results from the study supported the hypothesis that self-efficacy expectations are related to academic performance, vocational interests, and range of perceived career options. Additionally, self-efficacy significantly predicted academic persistence.

Many studies consistently have linked efficacy expectations to decision-making processes vital to choosing a math/science related college major (Eccles, 1994; Fassinger, 1990; Lapan & Jingeleski; 1992; Lapan, Shaughnessy, & Boggs, 1997; Lent, Brown, & Hackett, 1994, Lent & Hackett; 1987; Lent, Lopez, & Bieschke, 1993; Schaefers, Epperson, & Nauta, 1997). Betz and Hackett (1981) examined the relationship between self-efficacy and perceived career options for 134 female and 101 male undergraduates. Females reported high levels of self-efficacy for traditionally female occupations and lower levels of self-efficacy for non-traditional occupations. The researchers noted that interests, abilities, and values may impact women's self-efficacy expectations. Additionally, they believed that lack of experiences of successful accomplishments, lack of competent role models, and lack of encouragement from parents and teachers may also have influenced the young women's self-efficacy expectations and lack of perceived confidence in engineering, physical sciences, and mathematics.

Lent, Brown, and Larkin (1984) studied the relationships among self-efficacy, degree of persistence, and success in one's college major. The relation of self-efficacy expectations to academic persistence was studied in 42 students with science and engineering college majors. They found that students with higher self-efficacy expectations persisted longer in technical/scientific majors over the following year.

Factors related to persistence in engineering in 278 upper-level undergraduate women were also studied by Schaefers et al. (1997). Their study revealed that ability, self-efficacy, barriers to support, and interest congruence each significantly added to the model predicting persistence in STEM majors. Lapan et al. (1997) conducted a longitudinal study with 101 students prior to entering college and then again 3 years later after they had declared a major. Both math self-efficacy beliefs and vocational interest in mathematics were helpful in predicting entry into math/science majors, with men choosing significantly more STEM majors than women. Studying 197 women and men enrolled in university-level engineering/science programs, Hackett, Betz, Casas, and Rocha-Singh (1992) found that career self-efficacy (i.e., expectations of confidence in career related pursuits) was a strong predictor of college academic achievement for both men and women. Faculty encouragement and personal support were shown to be predictors of success for women and minorities in the sciences. The researchers suggested that attention to these predictors as well as proactive programs to increase self-efficacy and provide support to students underrepresented in the sciences should work to increase the probability for retention and success of these students.

Research has shown that gifted girls have higher grades than gifted boys throughout their school years. However, in the fourth and fifth grades, gifted boys begin to receive higher achievement test scores in math and science than do gifted girls. Despite their better grades, these lower achievement scores may erode young girls' beliefs in their own abilities (Robinson Kurpius & Kerr, 2001). Sadker and Sadker (1994) suggested that achievement test scores may have the largest impact on gifted girls' sudden plunge in self-esteem.

Gifted girls are also influenced by the culture of their families and surroundings. If gifted girls come from a traditional family or culture, they may be expected to leave behind their giftedness in adolescence (Kerr, 1997; Reis & Callahan, 1996). For example, they may feel free to pursue interests in science and math as a younger person but feel pressured later to conform to more traditionally female roles. Kitano (1996) noted that there is strong evidence that women who become high achievers in Latino and Asian cultures are those who receive extra encouragement from their families. Although intelligence in a girl is considered a positive characteristic until puberty (Kerr & Robinson Kurpuis, 1999), few cultures perceive intelligence as positive or attractive in women. Furthermore, men tend to marry their equals or inferiors in ability.

To help combat the many barriers to young women's achievement, in 1994 Kerr and Robinson Kurpius created a program entitled *Talented At-risk Girls: Encouragement and Training for Sophomores* (TARGETS) and in 1997 created a program entitled *Guiding Girls Into Math and Science* (GEMS). Funded by the National Science Foundation (NSF), these two programs were designed to help increase career aspirations in STEM fields and self-beliefs in talented at-risk high school girls. They studied over 500 girls and found that their intervention helped increase self-esteem, school-related self-efficacy (particularly math and science self-efficacy), and career search behaviors and decrease suicidality.

Despite various positive messages young gifted women may receive about their abilities, they often continue to struggle with self doubt. Some women who possess the necessary abilities to pursue a STEM major may later experience difficulties through the questioning of their own abilities. Clance and Imes (1978) described the "imposter phenomenon" as "the internal experience of intellectual phoniness" (p. 241). Additionally, Clance (1985) has stated, "Imposters believe they are intellectual frauds who have attained success because they were at the right place at the right time, knew someone in power, or simply were hard workers—never because they were talented or intelligent or deserved their positions" (p. 5). Often the imposter phenomenon occurs in young, highly intelligent women who may believe they have fooled everyone into thinking they are brighter than they really are (Gloria, 1993; Kerr, 1985). Researchers have hypothesized that women perceive a "chilly campus climate" that often does not foster their learning or respond to their needs and aspirations (Pascarella, Whitt, Edison, & Nora, 1997; Whitt, Edison, Pascarella, Nora, & Terenzini, 1999) The imposter phenomenon may become especially salient in young, intelligent women interested in STEM fields as their classes become more challenging and they are subjected to "chilly," male-focused classrooms. Blatant and covert societal messages regarding what women can and cannot do likely impact the way young women view themselves. Young talented women may perceive themselves as imposters if they are achieving in a STEM field that has been traditionally the domain of men. Self-beliefs, including self-esteem and educational self-efficacy, seem to have a strong impact on the likelihood that women will persist and achieve in non-traditional STEM fields. For highly intelligent women who are accomplished in a chosen field, negative views about themselves and their abilities may be expressed through feeling like an imposter. The role of self-esteem and educational self-efficacy continue to be important areas of study for understanding the barriers related to women's success in STEM majors and careers.

College Environment

For young women, the college experience may be marked by increased stress in both social and academic areas. For many, the beginning of college signifies a time in which they are letting go of day-to-day support from their families and high school friends. Compas, Wagner, Slavin, and Vannatta (1986) noted that, "Leaving home and entering college involves academic and social demands hypothesized to be a source of substantial risk and vulnerability" (p. 243). Chickering (1969) suggested the college experience encompasses a critical developmental period for late adolescents and young adults. Developmental changes may be stressful and present periods of homesickness and loneliness (Cutrona, 1982). During the first weeks, months, and even years of college, some students may feel disconnected from other students and professors. Rotenberg (1998) noted that the process of social adjustment to college may be marked by a continued inability to develop relationships with other students and persistent feelings of general disconnectedness. Often, students blame their lack of connectedness to others on an unfriendly campus climate (Gloria et. al, 1999; Gloria & Robinson Kurpius, 1996; Hurtado & Carter, 1997). Students who feel connected to their college or university, however, tend to view the campus in a positive light (Lee, Keough, & Sexton, 2002). For example, students who have a strong sense of community on campus, perceive a high degree of support, involvement, and achievement in their college environment (Gloria et al., 1999; Pretty, 1990).

In addition to changes in available social support resources, young women in a new college environment face confusing decisions about their futures that include choosing a major and eventually a career. Researchers have identified external barriers to women's persistence and achievement in STEM majors (Schaefers et al., 1997). External barriers are described as "hurdles imposed by societal sex role expectations and characteristics of the environment" (Schaefers et al., p 174). These barriers may include components such as lack of support from the educational environment and its faculty (Betz, 1994; Betz & Fitzgerald, 1987) and competitiveness in classroom and occupational settings (Eccles, 1987, McDade, 1988). Researchers suggest that women may leave STEM fields because they are less likely than men to receive support for pursuing non-traditional careers from both within and outside of the academic environment (Betz, 1994; Betz & Fitzgerald, 1987). Barriers to women's achievement in STEM majors may include a less than favorable "institutional climate" (Erhart & Sandler, 1987).

Excessive pressure on women seems to exist in many STEM environments on the college campus. For example, engineering programs are notoriously stressful and are known for the pressures they place on their students (Greenfield, Holloway, & Remus, 1982). Betz and Fitzgerald (1987) suggested that women often receive little support, if not direct discouragement, from pursuing nontraditional careers like engineering. Based on Bandura's (1982) argument that verbal encouragement and lower levels of anxiety are two important sources of efficacy information, Hackett et al. (1992) suggested that stress experienced by engineering students might be a factor in lowered academic and career self-efficacy. Freeman (1979) identified the "null environment hypothesis" that encompasses lack of support in the form of absence of encouragement and positive feedback from faculty members. Subsequently, the null environment hypothesis has been shown to be a significant barrier to women's educational advancement in non-traditional career areas (Hackett et al.). Given that university environments often reflect the values and perspectives of the White, male, middle class (Beauboeuf-Lafontant & Augustine, 1996; Feagin, Vera, & Imani, 1996), students with different perspectives may be forced to compromise parts of themselves or in order to succeed in the academic realm (Cervantes, 1988).

The climate of the STEM classroom seems to be significantly related to women's achievement and persistence in these fields. Griffin-Pierson (1998) suggested that women may be more likely than men to respond negatively to highly competitive environments such as those that often permeate the STEM classroom. In recent years, researchers and educators alike have been striving to find the best types of classroom environments that will foster women's development in STEM. Buncick, Betts, and Horgan (2001) suggested that "inclusivity," meaning all students are actively engaged in a classroom, is vital to student success. They wrote, "When the classroom is dominated by a few students (who may appear to be the only ones truly "getting it"), others may conclude that they must not be cut out for science" (p.1238). Buncick et al. asserted that environments in which some students feel excluded have been associated with attrition among students, especially those who are traditionally under-represented in science and engineering majors, including women, African Americans, Latinos, and Native Americans. In order for women to pursue STEM majors successfully, the college environment, including both social and academic realms, must be taken into consideration.

Talented Women and STEM

Although there are many math-science talented women attending college, these women often shy away from STEM majors. Academic ability has been shown to be positively related to persistence in non-traditional majors (Benbow & Arjmand, 1990) and non-traditional career choices (Eccles & Howard, 1993; Fassinger, 1990; Obrien & Fassinger, 1993) for women. However, Schaefers et al. (1997) noted that math/science ability alone does not fully account for gender differences in persistence and success in STEM fields. Sanders, Benbow, and Albright (1993) suggested that even women with outstanding mathematical ability are under-represented in college math and science majors as compared to their equally-talented male peers. In addition, sometimes female students who change from engineering to other college majors have higher grade point averages (GPA) than do men who continue to pursue engineering majors (Mead, 1991). Studying factors related to women's persistence in engineering majors, Schaefers et al. found that a measure of ability, specifically first semester grade point average (GPA), made the strongest contribution to the model of persistence. The researchers suggested that deficiencies in ability, academic preparation, or work habits linked with lack of persistence in engineering majors may be apparent early in college women's experiences. Thus, the first semesters may be an ideal time for early assessment and intervention with hopes of increasing female persistence in the STEM fields.

Multipotentiality

In addition to ability, multipotentiality is a construct that has been shown to be central to some theories of career choice for the academically talented (Colangelo & Zaffrann, 1979; Kerr, 1981, 1990; Rysiew, Shore, & Carson, 1994). The term multipotentiality has been used by some researchers in the giftedness field to signify multiple abilities (Davis & Rim, 1986; Frederick, 1972). Conversely, Erlich (1982) stressed the significance of multiple interests as central to multipotentiality. More recently, researchers have emphasized both multiple abilities and multiple interests (Berger, 1989; Kerr, 1991; Sajjadi, Rejskind, & Shore, 2001; Silverman, 1993). Some giftedness researchers have linked multipotentiality to career indecision when four key variables—abilities, motivation, interests, and opportunity—exist. They believe that the "overchoice syndrome" that talented students often experience leads to difficulty in choosing a clear career path (Rysiew et al.). Often, academically talented students are told they can "do anything." They may stand out in a variety of subjects and because of a lack of any weaknesses, their true strengths and passions may be difficult to distinguish. When gifted and talented students are faced with the option of choosing among many interesting careers in which they may excel, decision-making becomes complex. Thus, the multipotentialed may waver among many available career options (Rysiew, Shore, & Leeb, 1999).

Kerr (1981; 1990; 1991) has suggested that many of the difficulties that gifted youth encounter in career decision-making may in part be due to multipotentiality. She categorized career decision-making obstacles into three areas: (a) making a single career choice in spite of multipotentiality, (b) making long-range career plans before having an adequate amount of emotional maturity, and (c) reconciling personal career goals with social expectations. These obstacles may be particularly pertinent to talented women interested in STEM careers. First, a gifted woman often may be exposed to many possible career options through suggestions from teachers, encouragement from an honors program, or even her own self-awareness that she holds talents in many areas. Next, a woman interested in a STEM career may know intellectually that she wants to pursue a career of this nature but may not be adequately prepared emotionally for the challenges and length of time it may take to pursue such a career. In addition, she may be, for the first time in her life, surrounded by many other gifted and talented women and men fighting for the same career dream. Finally, a woman desiring a career in a STEM field often receives both subtle and overt messages from family, friends, and even faculty that she is pursing a non-traditional path. She may prematurely begin to worry about the future and her ability to juggle family, friends, and career.

Researchers suggest that for students with high-ability, selection of a career may be an existential dilemma and even a form of an identity crisis (Perrone & Van Den Heuvel, 1981; Silverman, 1993). Because of pressures to achieve, an extremely bright woman may feel burdened by her academic strengths. Furthermore, her strong intelligence in multiple areas may compel her to feel as if she must achieve some degree of greatness by choosing the "perfect" career that will accomplish both her need to meet her potential as well as her need to contribute positively to society. The gifted girl tends to see a vocation as more than just a way to make a living (Carroll, Paine, & Miner, 1973). She may place a high value on being able to show self-expression and her philosophy of life, as well as exert many of her skills and talents through her career (Cornell, Robinson, & Ward, 1991; Yankelovich). The gifted woman may also exhibit her multipotentiality through excessive involvement in after school activities and through difficulty making decisions about colleges and career paths (Robinson Kurpius & Kerr, 2001).

Some researchers (Milgram & Hong, 1999; Sajjadi et al., 2001) have suggested that multipotentiality may not be problematic. They posited that multipotentiality may even be seen in positive terms as making one "highly adaptable" and likely to lead a varied and full life. Similarly, Kerr (1981) reported that multipotentiality is problematic only for those gifted people who view their career plans as out of control and cannot seem to find a way to integrate a diverse set of interests and abilities. For young, gifted women, multipotentiality may become a problem for those perplexed individuals who visit an academic or career counselor only to hear a well-meaning "You can be anything you want to be!" (Kerr & Erb, 1991). Rysiew et al. (1999) suggested that for gifted students exhibiting multipotentiality, self-exploration beyond interests and abilities is imperative.

For women in an undergraduate honors program and interested in STEM careers, multipotentiality may take on added meaning. Most often these women hold multiple talents in various academic fields. In order to be admitted to an Honors program, they must perform well across a variety of disciplines. They may often hear statements that imply they can "do anything." Furthermore, as women interested in a career in STEM, they are likely in a non-traditional field and in preparation courses where there is significant under-representation of women. For the gifted and talented women interested in STEM, the social and intellectual challenges they face may exacerbate problems of multipotentiality. They may in some sense "take advantage" of their status as a mutipotentialed individual and pursue a potential outside of STEM, failing to realize fully their true career goals and dreams.

Career Goals

Clearly defined career goals have been found to be significantly related to retention (Tinto, 1993) and seem to impact positively retention related to persistence in STEM majors and careers (Kerr & Robinson Kurpius, 2000; Robinson Kurpius & Kerr, 2001). Career goals may also provide a booster to retention-related factors such as academic performance, self-beliefs, and commitment to school and career (Hull-Blanks et al., 2004). For example, Altmaier, Rapaport, and Seeman (1983) reported that students' ambivalence about career goals strongly impacted poor academic performance. Conversely, Ting (1997) found that the presence of long-term goals significantly predicted academic performance.

Career goals have also been found to be related to self-esteem and educational self-efficacy. For example, Nauta, Epperson, and Kahn (1998) reported that higher self-esteem predicted career aspirations of female STEM majors. Similarly, female college students who aspired to career goals in science and math scored higher on self-esteem measures than did those who sought homemaking occupations. Hackett et al., (1989) studied only women and found that performance self-esteem was predictive of both higher educational aspirations and career salience. Furthermore, Hackett and Betz (1981) found that women's self-efficacy is related to increased choice of career goals. For women interested in STEM majors and careers, it is essential that career goals are an area of consideration.

Role Models and Mentors

Having role models and mentors is an important way to increase persistence in STEM majors. Leppel (2001) used national data to analyze the impact of majors on college persistence among freshmen. She suggested that mentors of the same sex as the student could be especially helpful in protecting against negative effects of social stereotypes. Chang (2002) compiled research from the National Science Foundation (NSF) and the National Science Board (NSB) and found that mentoring programs that help socialize students to STEM fields and can be an integral form of support for women and minorities.

Mentors may also provide women interested in science with a support network that works to increase self-confidence and feelings of connectedness to the field (Goodman Research Group, 2002). Furthermore, NSF (1996) asserted that guidance from faculty or peer mentors has been shown to have a significant impact on retention in the sciences. Mentors may also have a positive impact on how students perceive the university experience. Pancer et al. (2000) studied 226 students' expectations about university life and subsequent adjustments in the first year. They found that students who had more complex expectations about university life tended to adjust better to stressful university situations than did students with simpler expectations. For example, students with complex expectations about university life may not be as likely to feel disappointed by unmet expectations. Since they anticipate possible challenges and difficulties, they may have developed coping strategies to combat them. Conversely, students with simpler expectations about university life may not be ready for the challenges they will inevitably face in a university setting. The researchers suggested that the most effective intervention programs would be those that prepare students for some of the obstacles they may face while attending the university and provide them with strategies to combat those difficulties.

Summary

Although female enrollment in law, medicine, and business has increased significantly, women are still underrepresented in the STEM fields (NSB, 2002; NSF, 1996; 2000). There is evidence to suggest that choices of college majors are not entirely based on individual aptitudes and interests (Eccles, 1994). Many factors including educational and personal self-efficacy, self-esteem, at-risk status, college environment, multipotentiality, and lack of female role models seem to influence women's motivation and choice to enter into a STEM major. Compared to men, the number of women who attempt STEM majors, especially engineering majors (NSB, 2002; NSF, 2000), is extremely low. Interventions that aim at the specific needs of women are clearly necessary.

The first year of college is a critical time for students (Tinto, 1982; 1993). For many, the transition away from home, high school, and the comforts of a familiar environment may prove difficult. Life at college presents a variety of responsibilities and demands and requires a high level of self-regulation (Bryde & Milburn, 1990). Tinto (1993, 1997) stressed the importance of integrating social and academic realms when trying to foster college persistence. In college, it may be more difficult to find concentrated areas of support and a sense of belongingness. "The academic major represents an important source of identity for students and is the only institutionally provided peer group that is academically based" (Terenzini & Wright, 1987, p. 177). For young women interested in STEM, the peer group associated with their academic majors may likely be perceived at best as a group they cannot relate to, and at worst, unsupportive or discouraging.

Kerr and Robinson Kurpius (2000) pointed out that "most career development interventions continue to treat women's career decisions as choices made in isolation from other choices such as the decision to marry or have children. For career counseling strategies to be effective, it is necessary that vocational planning take place within the larger context of life planning" (pp. 1-2). For academically talented women, the decision to persist in a STEM major may be one of the first issues impacted by the pressures related to the transition to college. Interventions that occur prior to and during students' first semester in school may be particularly helpful in increasing persistence rates for women in STEM majors (Schaefers et al., 1997).

References:

American Association of University Women. (1991). *Shortchanging girls, shortchanging America.* Washington, DC: AAUW.

Altmaier, E., Rapaport, R., & Seeman, D. (1983). A needs assessment of liberal arts students on academic probation. *Journal of College Student Personnel, 24*(3), 266-267.

Bandura, A. (1977). Self-efficacy: Toward a unifying theory of behavioral change. *Psychological Review, 84*(2), 191-215.

Bandura, A. (1982). Self-efficacy mechanisms in human agency. *American Psychologist, 37,* 122-147.

Beauboeuf-Lafontant, T. D., & Augustine, D. S. (Eds.). (1996). *Facing racism in education.* (2nd ed.). Cambridge, MA: Harvard Educational Review.

Beauvais, F. (1992). The consequences of drug and alcohol use for Indian youths. *American Indian and Alaska Native Mental Health Research, 5*(1), 32-37.

Benbow, C. P., & Arjmand, O. (1990). Predictors of high academic achievement in mathematics and science by mathematically talented students: A longitudinal study. *Journal of Educational Psychology, 82,* 430-441.

Bennett, C., & Okinaka, A. M. (1990). Factors related to persistence among Asian, Black, Hispanic, and White undergraduates at a predominately White university: Comparison between first and fourth year cohorts. *The Urban Review, 22*(1), 33-60.

Betz, N. E. (1994). Career counseling for women in the sciences and engineering. In W. B. Walsh & S. H. Osipow (Eds.), *Career counseling for women* (pp. 237-261). Hillsdale, NJ: Erlbaum.

Betz, N. E., & Fitzgerald, L. F. (1987). Personality variables and women's career development: Self-concept and sex role-related characteristics. In N.

E. Betz (Ed.), *The career psychology of women* (pp. 112-128). New York: Academic Press.

Betz, N. E., & Hackett, G. (1981). The relationship of career related self-efficacy expectations to perceived career options in college women and men. *Journal of Counseling Psychology, 28,* 399-410.

Betz, N. E., & Hackett, G. (1983). The relationship of mathematics self-efficacy expectations to the selection of science-based college majors. *Journal of Vocational Behavior, 23,* 329-345.

Boulter, L.T. (2002). Self-concept as a predictor of college freshman academic adjustment. *College Student Journal, 36*(2), 234-246.

Brown, L., & Gilligan, C. (1992). *At the crossroads.* Cambridge, MA: Harvard University Press.

Bryde, J. F., & Milburn, C. M. (1990). Helping to make the transition from high school to college. In R. L. Emans (Ed.), *Understanding undergraduate education.* Vermillion, SD: University of South Dakota Press.

Buncick, M. C., Betts, P. G., Horgan, D. D. (2001). Using demonstrations as a contextual road map: Enhancing course continuity and promoting active engagement in introductory college physics. *International Journal of Science Education, 23*(12), 1237-1255.

Campbell, P., & Clewell, B. C. (1999). Science, math, and girls: Still a long way to go. *Education Week,* p.50.

Cervantes, R. C. (1988). Hispanics in psychology. In P. J. Woods (Ed.), *Is psychology for them? A guide for undergraduate advising.* (pp. 182-184). Washington, DC: American Psychological Association.

Chang, J. C. (2002). *Women and minorities in the science, mathematics and engineering pipeline* (Report No. EDO-JC-02-06). Washington, DC: Office of Educational Research and Improvement.

(ERIC Document Reproduction Service No. ED467855).

Chickering, A. W. (1969). *Education and identity.* San Francisco: Jossey Bass.

Clance, P. R. (1985). *The imposter phenomenon.* Atlanta, GA: Peachtree Press.

Clance, P. R., & Imes, S. A. (1978).The imposter phenomenon in high achieving women: Dynamics and therapeutic intervention. *Psychotherapy: Theory, Research and Practice, 15*(3), 241-247.

Compas, B. E., Wagner, B. M., Slavin, L.A., & Vanatta, K. (1986). A prospective study of life events, social support, and psychological symptomatology during the transition from high school to college. *American Journal of Community Psychology, 14,* 241-257.

Cutrona, C. E. (1982). Transition to college: Loneliness and the process of social adjustment. In L. A. Peplau & D. Perlman (Eds.), *Loneliness: A sourcebook of current theory, research, and therapy,* (pp. 291-309). New York: Wiley.

Daugherty, T. K., & Lane, E. J. (1999). A longitudinal study of academic and social predictors of college attrition. *Social Behavior and Personality, 27*(4), 355-362.

Duke, L. (2002). Get Real!: Cultural relevance and resistance to the mediated feminine ideal. *Psychology and Marketing, 19*(2), 211-233.

Dweck, C. (1995). *Students' theories about their intelligence: Implications for the gifted.* Paper presented at the Rosen National Symposium on Gifted Education, Lawrence, KS.

Eccles, J. S. (1994). Understanding women's educational and occupational choices. *Psychology of Women Quarterly, 18,* 585-609.

Eccles, J. S., & Harold, R. D. (1992). Gender differences in educational and occupational patterns among the gifted. In N. Colangelo, S. G. Assouline, & D. L.

Ambroson (Eds.), *Talent development.* Scottsdale, AZ: Great Potential Press.

Erhart, J., & Sandler, B. R. (1987*). Looking for more than just a few good women in traditionally male fields.* Washington, DC: Project on the Status and Education of Women.

Ethier, K., & Deaux, K. (1990). Hispanics in ivy: Assessing identity and perceived threat. *Sex Roles, 22,* 427-440.

Fassinger, R. E. (1990). Causal models in career choices in two samples of college women. *Journal of Vocational Behavior, 36,* 225-248.

Feagin, J. R., Vera, H., & Imani, N. (1996). *The agony of education: Black students at White colleges and universities.* New York: Routledge.

Felton, G. M., & Bartoces, M. (2002). Predictors of initiation of early sex in Black and White adolescent females. *Public Health Nursing, 19*(1), 59-67.

Freeman, J. (1979). How to discriminate against women without really trying. In J. Freeman (Ed.), *Women: A feminist perspective* (2nd ed., pp. 217-232). Palo Alto, CA: Mayfield.

Gagliardi, C. J, Gloria, A. M., Robinson Kurpius, S. E., & Lambert, C. D. (2004). In D. Capuzzi & D. R. Gross (Eds.). *Youth at Risk: A prevention resource for counselors, teachers, and parents* (4th ed., pp. 373-400). Alexandria, VA: American Counseling Association.

Gloria, A. M. (1993). Psychosocial factors influencing the academic persistence of chicano/a undergraduates. . *Dissertations Abstracts International, 54 (11-A),* 4001.

Gloria, A. M., & Robinson Kurpius, S. E. (2001). Influences of self-beliefs, social support, and comfort in the university environment on the academic nonpersistence decisions of American Indian undergraduates. *Cultural Diversity and Ethnic Minority Psychology, 7*(1), 88-102.

Gloria, A. M., & Robinson Kurpius, S. E. (1999). African American students' persistence at a predominately white university: Influences of social support, university comfort, and self-beliefs. *Journal of College Student Development, 40*(3), 257-268.

Goodman Research Group. (2002). *Final report of the women's experiences in college engineering (WECE) project.* Cambridge, MA.

Greenfield, L. B., Holloway, E.L., & Remus, L. (1982). Women students in engineering: Are they so different from men? *Journal of College Student Personnel, 23,* 508-514.

Griffin-Pierson, S. (1988). A new conceptualization of competitiveness in women. Unpublished doctoral dissertation, University of Iowa, Iowa City.

Hackett, G., & Betz, N. (1981). A self-efficacy approach to the career development of women. *Journal of Vocational Behavior, 18,* 326-329.

Hackett, G., Betz, N. E., Casas, J. M., & Rocha-Singh, I. A. (1992). Gender, ethnicity, and social cognitive factors in predicting the academic achievement of students in engineering. *Journal of Counseling Psychology, 39*(4), 527-538.

Hackett, G., Betz, N. E., Esposito, D., & O'Halloran, M. S. (1989). The relationship of role model influence to the career salience and educational career plans of college women. *Journal of Vocational Behavior, 35*(2), 164-180.

Harper, G., & Robinson, W. (1999). Pathways to risk among inner-city African American adolescent females: The influence of gang membership. *American Journal of Community Psychology, 27*(3), 383-404.

Hart, S. (2000). *Adolescent Risk Behavior: Their effects of parent, older siblings, and peers.* Unpublished doctoral dissertation, Arizona State University.

Hartman, I. S. (1995). AIM: Attracting women into sciences. *Journal of Chemical Education, 72*, 711.

Hollinger, C., & Fleming, E. (1984). Internal barriers to the realization of potential: correlates and interrelationships among gifted and talented female adolescents. *Gifted Child Quarterly, 28*(3), 135-139.

Hull-Blanks, E., Robinson Kurpius, S. E., Befort, M. C., Sollenberger, S., Foley Nicpon, M., Huser, L. (2004). Career goals and retention-related factors among college freshmen. *Journal of Career Development.*

Hurtado, S., & Carter, D. F. (1997). Effects of college transition and perceptions of the campus racial climate on Latino college students' sense of belonging. *Sociology of Education, 70,* 324-345.

Johnson, G. M. (1994). Undergraduate student attrition: A comparison of the characteristics of students who withdraw and students who persist. *Alberta Journal of Educational Research, 40,* 337-353.

Jourard, S. M. (1974). *Healthy Personality: An approach from the viewpoint of Humanistic psychology.* New York: MacMillan:

Kenny, L. D. (2000). *Daughters of Suburbia: Growing up White, middle-class and female.* New Brunswick, NJ: Rutgers University Press.

Kerr, B. A. (1981). *Career education for the gifted and talented.* Columbus, OH: National Center for Research in Vocational Education. (ERIC Document Reproduction Service No. ED 205 778).

Kerr, B. A. (1985). *Smart girls, gifted women.* Dayton, Ohio: Ohio Psychology Press.

Kerr, B.A. (1985). Smart girls, gifted women: Counseling gifted persons: A lifelong concern. *Roeper-Review, 8*(1), 30-33.

Kerr, B. A. (1990). *Career planning for gifted and talented youth.* Reston, VA: Council for Exceptional Children, ERIC Clearinghouse on Handicapped and Gifted Children. (ERIC Document Reproduction Service No. ED 321 497).

Kerr, B. A. (1994). *Smart girls two: A new psychology of girls, gifted women, and giftedness.* Dayton, Ohio: Ohio Psychology Press.

Kerr, B. A. (1997). *Smart girls: A new psychology of girls, women, and giftedness.* Scottsdale, AZ: Gifted Psychology Press.

Kerr, B. A., & Erb, C. A. (1991). Career counseling with academically talented students: Effects of a value-based intervention. *Journal of Counseling Psychology, 38*(3), 309-314.

Kerr, B. A., & Foley Nicpon, M. (2003). Gender and giftedness. In N. Colangelo & G. A. Davis (Eds.), *Handbook of Gifted Education* (3rd ed.). Boston, MA: Allyn & Bacon.

Kerr, B. A. & Robinson Kurpius, S. E. (1999). Brynhilde's Fire: Talent, risk and betrayal in the lives of gifted girls. In J. LeRoux (Ed.), *Connecting the gifted community worldwide* (pp. 261-271). Ottawa: World Council on Gifted and Talented.

Kerr, B. A. & Robinson Kurpius, S. E. (1997). *Guiding Girls into Math and Science (GEMS).* Grant funded by the National Science Foundation.

Kerr, B. A. & Robinson Kurpius, S. E. (1994). *Talented At Risk Girls: Encouragement and Training for Sophomores (TARGETS).*Grant funded by the National Science Foundation.

Kitano, M. K., & Perkins, C. O. (1996). International gifted women: Developing a critical resource. *Roeper Preview, 19*(1), 34-30.

Lapan, R. T., & Jingeleski, J. (1992). Circumscribing vocational aspirations in junior high school. *Journal of Counseling Psychology, 39*, 81-90.

Lapan, R. T., Shaughnessy, P., & Boggs, K. (1996). Efficacy expectations and vocational interests as mediators between sex and choice of math/ science college majors: A longitudinal study. *Journal of Vocational Behavior, 49*, 277-291.

Lea-Wood, S. S., & Clunies-Ross, G. (1995). Self-esteem of gifted adolescent girls in Australian schools. *Roeper Review, 17,* 195-197.

Lee, R. M., Keough, K. A., & Sexton, J. D. (2002). Social connectedness, social appraisal, and perceived stress in college women and men. *Journal of Counseling and Development, 80,* 355-361.

Lent, R.W., Brown, S. D., & Larkin, K.C. (1984). Relation of self-efficacy expectations to academic achievement and persistence. *Journal of Counseling Psychology, 31,* 356-362.

Lent, R.W., Brown, S. D., & Larkin, K.C. (1986). Self-Efficacy in the prediction of academic performance and perceived career options. *Journal of Counseling Psychology, 33,* 265-269.

Lent, R. W., & Hackett, G. (1987). Career self-efficacy: Empirical status and future directions. *Journal of Vocational Behavior, 30,* 347-382.

Lent, R. W., Lopez, F. G., & Bieschke, K. J. (1993). Predicting mathematics-related choice and success behaviors: Test of an expanded social cognitive model. *Journal of Vocational Behavior, 42,* 223-236.

Lent, R. W., Brown, S. D., & Hackett, G. (1994). Toward a unifying social cognitive theory of career and academic interest, choice, and performance. *Journal of Vocational Behavior, 45,* 79-122.

Leppel, K. (2001). The impact of major on college persistence among freshmen. *Higher Education, 41,* 327-342.

Luzzo, D. A., & McWhirter, E. H. (2001). Sex and ethnic differences in the perception of educational and career-related barriers and levels of coping efficacy. *Journal of Counseling and Development, 79,* 61-67.

Meade, J. (1991). The missing piece. *ASEE Prism, 1,* 19-22.

Milgram, R. M. & Hong, E. (1999). Multipotential abilities and vocational interests in gifted adolescents: Fact or fiction? *International Journal of Psychology, 34*(2), 81-93.

National Science Board (2002). *Science and engineering indicators-2002*, (Report No. NSB-02-1). Arlington, VA: Author.

National Science Foundation (1996). *Women, minorities, and persons with disabilities in science and engineering: 1996* (Report No. NOS 96-311). Arlington, VA: Author. (ERIC Document Reproduction Service Number ED 402 192).

National Science Foundation (2000). *Women, minorities, and persons with disabilities in science and engineering: 2000* (Report No. NSF 00-327). Arlington, VA. (ERIC Document Reproduction Service Number ED 128 764).

Nauta, M. M., Epperson, D. L., & Kahn, J. H. (1998). A multiple groups analysis of predictors of higher-level career aspirations among women in mathematics, sciences and engineering majors. *Journal of Counseling Psychology, 45*(4), 483-496.

O'Brien, K. M., & Fassinger, R. E. (1993). A causal model of the career orientation and career chose of adolescent women. *Journal of Counseling Psychology, 40*, 456-469.

Orenstein, P. (1994). *School Girls: Young women, self-esteem, and the confidence gap.* New York: Doubleday.

Pancer, S. M., Hunsberger, B., Pratt, M. W., & Alisat, S. (2000). Cognitive complexity of expectations and adjustment to university in the first year. *Journal of Adolescent Research, 15*(1), 38-57.

Pascarella, E. T., Whitt, E. J., Edison, M. I., & Nora, A. (1997). Women's perceptions of a "chilly climate" and their cognitive outcomes during the first years of college, *Journal of College Student Development, 38*(2), 109-124.

Phillips, L. (1998). *The girls report—What we know and need to know about growing up female.* New York: The Report of the National Council for Research on Women.

Pipher, M. (1994). *Reviving Ophelia: Saving the selves of adolescent girls.* New York: Ballantine Books.

Pretty, G. M. H. (1990). Relating psychological sense of community to social climate characteristics. *Journal of Community Psychology, 18,* 60-65.

Rayle, A. D., Arredondo, P., & Robinson Kurpius, S. E. (in press). Educational self-efficacy of college women: Implications for theory, research, and practice. *Journal of Counseling and Development.*

Reis, S., &, Callahan, C. M. (1996). My boyfriend, my girlfriend, or me: The dilemma of talented teenage girls. *Journal of Secondary Education, 2,* 434-445.

Rosenberg, M., Schooler, C., Schoenbach, C., & Rosenberg, F. (1995). Global self-esteem and specific self-esteem: Different concepts, different outcomes. *American Sociological Review, 60*(1), 141-156.

Robinson Kurpius, S. E. (2002). *Psychosocial Factors in the Lives of College Freshmen, Vice Presidential Address,* Paper presented at the American Educational Research Association Annual Conference, New Orleans, LA.

Robinson Kurpius, S. E., Payakakkom, A., & Chee, C. (2004). *Psychometric properties of measure of self-beliefs for Latino, Native American, and Euro-American undergraduates.* Paper presented at the Relevance in Assessment of Culture and Evaluation Annual Conference, Tempe, AZ

Robinson Kurpius, S. E., Dixon Rayle, A., Arredondo, P., Tovar-Gamero, A., Bordes, V., Sand, J., Johnson, T., Payakakkom, A., & Chee, C. (2004). *Academic Persistence for College Freshmen: Factors that*

Matter for Ethnic/Racial Minority and Caucasian Students. Paper presented at the American Counseling Association Annual Meeting, Kansas City, KS.

Robinson Kurpius, S. E., Chee, C., Rayle, A., & Arredondo, P. (2003). *Academic persistence of Native American and Latino undergraduates: Psychosocial influences.* Paper presented at the National Association for College Admissions Counselors Annual Conference, Long Beach, CA.

Robinson Kurpius, S. E., & Kerr, B. A. (2001). *Guiding girls into engineering math and science.* Paper presented at the American Educational Research Association Annual Meeting, Seattle, WA.

Robinson Kurpius, S. E., Krause, S., Yasar, S, Roberts, C., & Baker, D. (2004). *Assessing DET in schools.* Paper presented at the National Association of Science Research in Teaching, Vancouver, Canada.

Rosenberg, M. (1965). *Society and the adolescent self-image.* Princeton, NJ: Princeton University Press.

Rosenberg, M. (2001). Self-concept research: A historical overview. *Social Forces, 68*(1), 34-44

Rosenberg, M., Schooler, C., Schoenbach, C., & Rosenberg, F. (1995). Global self-esteem and specific self-esteem: Different concepts, different outcomes, *American Sociological Review, 60*(1), 141-156.

Rotenberg, K. J. (1998). Stigmatization of transitions in loneliness. *Journal of Social and Personal Relationships, 15*, 565-576.

Rysiew, K. J., Shore, B. M., & Carson, A. D. (1994). Multipotentiality and overchoice syndrome: Clarifying common usage. *Gifted and Talented International, 9*,(2), 41-46.

Rysiew, K. J., Shore, B. M., & Leeb, R. T. (1999). Multipotentiality, giftedness, and career choice.

Journal of Counseling and Development, 77, 423-430.

Sadker, M., & Sadker, D. (1994). *Failing at fairness: How America's schools cheat girls.* New York: Charles Scribner's Sons.

Sajjadi, S. H., Rejskind, G., & Shore, B. M. (2001). Is multipotentiality a problem or not? A new look at the data. *High Ability Studies, 12*(1), 27-43.

Sanders, C. W., Benbow, C. P., & Albright, P. (1993). Mathematically talented females and their career decisions over a 10-year time-period. Unpublished manuscript.

Sebrechts, J., (1999). The women's college difference. In S. N. Davis, M. Crawford, & J. Sebrechts (Eds.), *Coming into her own: Educational success in girls and women* San Francisco, CA: Jossey-Bass.

Schaefers, K. G., Epperson, D. L., & Nauta, M. M. (1997). Women's career development: Can theoretically derived variables predict persistence in engineering majors? *Journal of Counseling Psychology, 44*(2), 173-183.

Seymour, E. (1992). "The problem iceberg" in science, mathematics, and engineering education: Student explanations for high attrition rates. *Journal of College Science Teaching, 2,* 230-238.

Seymour, E., & Hewitt, N. M. (1997). *Talking about leaving: Why undergraduates leave the sciences.* Boulder, CO: Westview Press.

Super, D. (1953). A theory of vocational development. In H.J. Peters & H. C. Hansen (Eds.), *Vocational guidance and career development.* London: Collier-Macmillan Ltd.

Super D., & Bohn, M. (1971). *Occupational psychology.* London: Tavistock.

Terenzini, P. T., & Pascarella, E. T. (1977). Voluntary freshman attrition and patterns of social and academic integration in a university: A test of a conceptual model. *Research in Higher Education, 6,* 25-43.

Terenzini, P. T., & Wright, T. M. (1987). Influences on students' academic growth during four years of college. *Research in Higher Education, 26*(2), 161-179.

Ting, S. (1997). Estimating academic success in the 1st year of college for specially admitted White students: A model combining cognitive and psychosocial predictors. *Journal of College Student Development, 38*(4), 401-409.

Tinto, V. (1982). Defining dropout: A matter of perspective. In E.T. Pascarella (Ed.), *Studying student attrition* (pp. 3-16). San Francisco: Jossey-Bass.

Tinto, V. (1993). *Leaving college: Rethinking the causes and cures of student attrition.* Chicago: The University of Chicago Press.

Tinto, V. (1997). "Classrooms as communities", *The Journal of Higher Education, 68*(6), 599-623.

Turner, S. E., & Bowen, W. G. (1999). Choice of major: the changing (unchanging) gender gap. *Industrial and Labor Relations Review, 52*(2), 289-313.

Upchurch, D. M., Aneshensel, C. S., Sucoff, C. A., & Levy-Storms, L. (1999). Neighborhood and family contexts of adolescent sexual activity. *Journal of Marriage and Family, 61*(4), 920-934.

Ware, N. C., & Lee, V. E. (1988). Sex differences in choice of college science majors. *American Educational Research Journal, 25*(4), 593-614.

Whitt, E. J., Edison, M. I., Pascarella, E. T., Nora, M., & Terenzini, P. T. (1999). Women's perceptions of a "chilly climate" and cognitive outcomes in college: Additional evidence. *Journal of College Student Development, 40*(2), 163-177.

Zimbardo, P. (1979). *Psychology and life.* (10th ed.) Glenview, Ill: Scott Foresman.

Zimmerman, B. J., Bandura, A., & Martinez-Pons, M. (1992). Self-motivation for academic attainment: The role of self-efficacy beliefs and personal goal setting. *American Educational Research Journal, 29*(3), 663-676.

Section 2

The Interventions

The four chapters in this section give an in-depth look into the particular interventions that seemed to make the TARGETS program for high school girls and its extension, the GEOS program for college women, so effective. First, a typical day at the TARGETS laboratory is described to give an overview and show how each intervention fits into the overall program. A comprehensive examination of the use of values clarification and future visualization in these workshops follows. Next, the use of the Vocational Preference Inventory in career assessment and the use of the Personality Research Form in personality assessment are explained.

3

Preserving the Promise: A Typical Day at TARGETS

Megan Nicpon Foley
Barbara Kerr

Imagine that you are a 15 year old girl who has never been chosen for any honor or recognition in your school. You feel bored a lot of time, and science and math classes are the only ones in which you feel challenged. Your grade point average is not so great, because although you get A's in math and science, you tend to blow off the other courses. You are not the prettiest or most popular girl in any group, and your slight accent still makes you feel a little uncomfortable about speaking out in class. You have some problems at home, so sometimes you hang out with older kids, doing the crazy things they do, just to get out of the house. You'd like to go to college, and you'd like to grow up to do something important – but you don't know what that would be, and you feel like there is too much standing in the way of ever getting there.

Imagine your surprise, when one day, out of the clear blue sky, your science teacher gives you a letter from Arizona State University saying that you have been selected for a program for gifted girls who are "at-risk" for not achieving their goals. On the one hand, you never thought of yourself as gifted. On the other hand, you secretly wonder if anyone really could do anything to help you overcome the things inside of you and all around you that keep you from believing in yourself. You are intrigued, and you decide to go.

When the sophomore high school girls arrive on the ASU campus around 8:30 a.m. in groups of 10 to 15, they have already completed a personality assessment, the *Personality Research Form* (Jackson, 1986), and are only aware that they were chosen to attend a workshop to learn more about themselves. As the girls are guided into the TARGETS meeting room, they encounter the TARGETS motto: Fun, food and friends. The walls are covered with brightly colored signs that say, "Welcome TARGETS," "Explore," and "Make Choices;" the table is piled with muffins and juices and TARGETS counselors are there to greet the girls with smiles and laughter. The girls begin to realize this is not going to be an ordinary school day when Drs. Kerr and Robinson Kurpius explain a TARGETS day. Each letter of the acronym is described in a way that is receptive and encouraging. The central message is that the girls are truly gifted and talented – someone has noticed—as well as likely to be experiencing some barriers to their goals. Again, someone has noticed.

After the introduction, the planned activities then begin with the girls drawing pictures that represent their views of who they are. Next, the girls are encouraged to share their pictures with the group as a way to gain an understanding of their individual uniqueness. The girls who are not yet ready to let strangers into their world are allowed to sit quietly and listen as the other girls tell their stories. When this activity is over, the girls complete the *Rokeach Values Survey* (Rokeach, 1982), pick their top three values, and present them for group discussion. As the sharing takes place, the girls begin to realize that while each girl has unique values, most of their values are quite similar. To make the atmosphere less tentative and tense, the TARGETS directors and counselors join in these discussions and share their values as a way of opening themselves up to the girls.

This activity is followed by a quick snack break and, after the break, the girls complete the *Math-Science Self-Efficacy Scale* (Robinson, 1992), the *Rosenberg Self-Esteem Inventory* (1965), and the *Vocational Preference Inventory* (Holland, 1988) for use in individual counseling sessions. They also provide demographic and family background information about their ethnicity, age, and family. Finally, the girls respond to questions about their career aspirations and the barriers they anticipate may prevent them from achieving their goals. Counselors are available at all times while the girls complete their questionnaires to provide assistance as well as positive feedback. Everything is done to make the process an enjoyable learning experience instead of a tedious task.

After all their tasks are completed, the girls are guided into the Counselor Training Center group therapy rooms. Once there, they relax in cozy, dimly lit rooms with big pillows and cushion seats for the Future Day Fantasy exercise. This experience is designed to have the girls project themselves 10 years into their futures. Two counselors lead the imagery by first helping the girls relax and focus inward. They are then asked to take a journey into what they would envision as a perfect career day 10 years into the future. Counselors guide the girls throughout their future career day by beginning in the morning and asking the girls to look around them, focusing on smells, sights and temperature. Then the girls are guided by the questions:

· What are you wearing?

87

- Where are you going?
- Does it take long to get there?
- What does the building look like?
- What do you do?
- Are there people?
- Animals?

These questions are designed to help the girls envision what their career days will be like. Last, the girls are asked to visualize going home and are walked through an evening at home. As their evening ends, the girls are asked to reflect on their day, focusing on how they felt and what was surprising about the experience.

Each girl then describes her experience to the group as the counselors write down the highlights. Usually the girls are quite excited about their future visions, and some describe future surprises. For example, many of the Native American girls from reservations say that in their dreams they were living in cities. For many of these girls this seems impossible because of their desire to stay on the reservation. It is a struggle for them to go after their dreams when they do not coincide with family and cultural expectations. As counselors, it is important to be aware of cultural realities of the girls, as well as to be supportive and encouraging about their dreams.

After the Future Day Fantasy, the girls go to lunch on ASU's campus. For most of them, this is their first time on a college campus. This too can serve as a motivator for the girls. For the first time, they walk among college buildings, professors, and students, feeling the excitement and newness of the college experience. Meanwhile, the TARGETS counselors are busy organizing the information each girl completed earlier for use in the individual counseling sessions. Each counselor is assigned two girls. They score all of the instruments that the girls previously completed, forming a conceptual understanding of each girl's interests, needs and values. Drs. Kerr and Robinson Kurpius consult with the counselors, helping to form an accurate picture of each girl. Some of the girls present as particularly at-risk. They may identify as having several barriers to reaching their goals (financial problems, lack of family support, etc.) or have personality profiles that indicate risky behaviors (expressing a high need for adventure and play or a low need for achievement, etc.). Above all, the emphasis of this session is to prepare the counselors to make the girls feel special and empowered, regardless of the preexisting barriers to their success.

When the girls return from lunch, half go directly to their individual counseling sessions, and the other half attend the at-risk group. The at-risk group is a meaningful part of the TARGETS day. The girls are given an at-risk questionnaire, the *Adolescent At-Risk Behaviors Inventory* (Robinson Kurpius, 1992), that consists of 27 items asking about their own risky behaviors (alcohol and drug usage, nutrition and exercise, smoking, sexual activity, birth control and AIDS, suicidal ideation). After they complete the questionnaire, counselors lead a frank, open discussion about these behaviors. The nonjudgmental atmosphere is helpful for the girls; for many, it may be the first time they are willing to talk with adults about their at-risk behaviors and the first time an adult has honestly and completely answered their questions. By disclosing in a group format, the girls become aware of the commonality of some struggles as well as learn ways to alter their actions to be more balanced and healthy.

During the at-risk group, the other half of the girls are in their individual counseling sessions. This is the highlight of the day for most of the girls and all of the counselors. It is designed to be the synthesis of the day; bringing all the information together for each girl in a warm, non-threatening environment. The session begins with the counselors asking the girls about themselves; questions about home, school, friends, and activities. Some of the sessions end here; that is, the girl is in need of help. Counselors have seen girls who are being abused, are severely into drugs or gang behavior, or suicidal. In these situations, it is imperative to work with the girl to ease the crisis. Referral information is given to identify available resources that can be utilized for further assistance. Drs. Kerr and Robinson Kurpius, who are psychologists, watch the counseling sessions through one-way mirrors and intervene if any girl is severely depressed or suicidal. Each girl has given her permission for her counseling session to be observed and has had a chance to see both sides of the one-way mirror.

For the majority of the girls who are not in crisis, the session moves into a discussion over the day. Counselors first reiterate to the girls why they were chosen to participate in a TARGETS day. Counselors reinforce that they too think that the girls are special and talented and that they can reach their dreams. The session flows into a discussion about the girl's interests, using results from the *Vocational Preference Inventory* (VPI) as a reference. The girls are exposed to the six areas of career interests in Holland's theory, and are asked which areas best describe them. The girls are then shown their VPI assessment results, and counselors assist the girls in comparing the test's interpretations to their own. Counselors expose the girls to careers from their VPI codes and explain to the girls that people who have interests similar to them are happy in these chosen fields. Frequently, the careers the girls identified on their demographic sheets somewhat match their VPI code. Counselors help the girls to see how their dream careers fit with their identified interests, as well as raise their career aspirations. For example, if a girl desires to be a nurse, the counselor asks whether the girl has thought about being a nurse practioner or a doctor.

Girls are then led into a discussion about their needs that help to shape their personalities. Counselors show the girls their *Personality Research Form* (PRF) profiles and ask if the results sound like them. For example, a counselor might say to a girl, "It seems that you have a high need for play, or a need to spend a lot of time doing things 'just for fun.' Does that sound like you?" It is important for the girls to know that having a high need or a low need for something does not equate to good or bad. For example, many of the girls have a high need for aggression. Counselors ask the girls how they can use this need in their careers, as well as how it could sometimes get in the way. Counselors help the girls to see how some needs that may appear to be destructive can be used instead as assets in career development.

After centering on the girls' needs, the counselors return to a discussion over the girls' values. The focus now is on the girls using their values within their careers. This leads directly into goal setting, where the girls verbalize and record goals to help them reach their eventual career dreams. Usually, the goals center on working harder in high school or finding out more information about college. The counselors' responsibility is to encourage the girls to set firm, reachable goals. They are briefly instructed on goal setting techniques; these girls most likely have experienced failures in the past and need to be familiarized with success. The girls are then promised that they will receive a letter from their counselor, asking them how they are progressing towards reaching this established goal.

After each girl has experienced both the at-risk group and an individual counseling session, the group comes together again for a final meeting. As the counselors hum "Pomp and Circumstance," each girl receives a hug, a smile and a Certificate of Completion that indicated that they are now graduates of the TARGETS program. The room is full of cheers and smiles from both girls and counselors; it is always a moment to remember. As the girls leave to go back to their homes, the counselors give their girls' hugs, promising again that they will be writing soon.

After the girls have left, the counselors meet together to discuss the experience. The day ends with a feeling of peace and hope that their efforts have changed at least one girl's life for the better.

About two or three weeks after a TARGETS day, counselors write their girls with hopes of getting a letter in return. The letters always reiterate how special the girls are and how wonderful it was to spend time with each one. Often, the girls write back, expressing wonderful, encouraging thoughts such as, "Thank you for being such a good friend to me," "Thank you for believing in me when no one else has," and "Trust me, I'll make you proud." Now, ten years after the first group of girls came to ASU, many TARBETS girls, now in college or graduate school, stay in touch with the counselors who first believed in them.

Approximately three months after the TARGETS day on-campus, a visit is made to the girls at their home schools. Not only are follow-up data collected, but it is a chance to do a booster session with the girls. This visit often results in even more meaningful conversations with the girls who are now comfortable with the directors of the project and are more than willing to share what is happening in their lives, particularly as it relates to school and their future.

References

Holland, J. L. (1988). *The Vocational Preference Inventory.* Odessa, FL: Psychological Assessment Resources.

Jackson, D. N. (1989). *The Personality Research Form.* Port Huron, MI: Research Psychologists Press.

Robinson, S. E. (1992a). *Adolescent At-Risk Behaviors Inventory.* Unpublished test. Tempe, AZ: Arizona State University.

Robinson, S. E. (1992b). *Educational Self-Efficacy Scale-Adolescents.* Unpublished test. Tempe, AZ: Arizona State University.

Rokeach, M. (1967). *Value Survey.* Palo Alto, CA: Consulting Psychologists Press.

Rosenberg, M. (1965). *Society and the adolescent self-image.* Princeton, NJ: Princeton University Press.

4

Making Dreams Come True
"What Will My Future Hold?"

Katherine Vaughn Fielder

There are many approaches to career counseling—
some very effective and some not so effective. This
chapter reviews the most common approaches to career
counseling and illustrates some of the limitations they
have when working with bright girls.

Traditional Approaches to Career Guidance Counseling

Few can argue the importance of effective career
guidance counseling in preparing bright girls for their
futures. Typically career counseling is based on five basic
approaches. Each has its strengths and limitations. The
most common model is a trait-and-factor approach in
which one takes several psychological assessments to
determine abilities, interests, and skills. Counselors then
compare these characteristics with those of people who
are happy and successful working in various occupational
environments. Satisfying careers are built from a good fit
or match between the girl's characteristics with the
environment's requirements. The focus in this type of

counseling is on making sound decisions and solving problems to help girls decide on a career that is both feasible and congruent with abilities, interests, and skills.

In **trait-and-factor career counseling**, the counselor acts primarily as an educator. The information provided is beneficial for girls, as it identifies broad areas of interests and can help shape a general area of focus or direction for future planning. Many of the popular career inventories based on trait-factor theory are biased toward males and present career options that frequently fall short of bright girls' aspirations. When used alone, this approach lacks the relationship and rapport elements found to be so important to teenage girls and found to be beneficial in the values-based career intervention developed through the TARGETS program.

The second type of career counseling is **psychodynamic.** Drawing upon principles developed in psycho-analytical therapy, the counselor emphasizes the internal forces that motivate the girl and the ways she copes in her environment. This information is then added to information attained through the trait-and-factor approaches described above. For bright girls, this approach has certain limitations. In order to reduce anxiety and increase decision making, this type of counseling often encourages girls to lower their career aspirations. By doing so it limits the number of career options available to them. It is important to counter the developmental crisis and resulting dumbing down in which so many bright adolescent girls engage. We need to focus on raising rather than lowering their career dreams. The **Perfect Future Day Fantasy** activity allows counselors to explore internal motivations (values) while simultaneously encouraging girls to raise their aspirations.

Another popular form of career guidance that is available to young women today is **person-centered**

counseling. The objective of client-centered work is to provide an environment that promotes the development of a self-concept that is compatible with a desired occupational role. The emphasis is not on decision making, but rather on accepting responsibility for making career decisions and feeling comfortable and confident in her choices. By taking a non-directive role, the counselor facilitates this process. As illustrated by career development theory, however, adolescent girls need structure and guidance as they explore their self-concepts and potential occupational roles. Adding the values component through the use of guided imagery is an appropriate method to do this.

The fourth approach to career guidance counseling is based on the developmental work of Super and is known as the **"life-span, life-space" approach to career guidance.** The counselor guides the client through a 4-phase assessment that evaluates the girl's developmental stage, her vocational identity that comprises her interests, skills, abilities, and values, and her self-concept and coping resources. The career intervention used in the TARGETS programs draws heavily from the developmental theory. Data are pulled together from a variety of assessments that examine a girl's self esteem, her interests, and her values. The **Future Day Fantasy** activity is a user-friendly activity that provides the means for a casual, yet in-depth interview containing many of the concepts emphasized in developmental theory.

The final approach to career guidance counseling is based on **social learning theory.** This approach examines how people choose their careers. Emphasis is placed on the process of learning career-related interests and how these determine career choice. This approach is most successful when working with clients who are struggling with specific career decisions. Examining irrational beliefs that impede one's career decisions and teaching clients to dispute the beliefs (e.g., financial constraints or gender bias) that prevent them from considering some careers is often beneficial. During the processing phase of future day fantasy activity, girls are encouraged to explore the barriers that might keep them from achieving their career dreams. Counselors can gently challenge irrational beliefs that emerge through use of cognitive restructuring techniques. Ideas developed through social learning theory are helpful in raising aspirations and exploring barriers to girls' career development.

Values in Career Counseling

TARGETS has drawn from the strengths of each of the above approaches to create a model of career intervention that encompasses a girl's developmental stage, her interests, her personal needs and values, her self-esteem, and her goals through a variety of written assessments and activities. This chapter focuses on values and dreams. We introduce the concept of values early in the day when the girls complete a version of the *Rokeach Values Inventory* that was specifically adapted for use with bright adolescent girls. The girls introduce themselves to the group by describing their "top" values. The emphasis on values continues during the **Perfect Future Day Fantasy** activity.

The Perfect Future Day Fantasy

The **Perfect Future Day Fantasy** is a simple and effective activity that enables counselors to incorporate the important aspects of career development theory succinctly while emphasizing the participant's values. The intervention uses structured guided imagery to facilitate career exploration, values clarification, and goal setting. Equally effective for males and females, the activity consists of two parts and takes approximately 50 minutes to one hour to complete. It can be done individually, in small groups, and in large groups.

The first part of the Fantasy consists of a guided imagery exercise. After an introduction to the activity, the facilitator begins the session by encouraging the girls to regulate their breathing, to relax their bodies, and to focus on the reader's voice. The girls are reminded that their bodies can become relaxed while their minds remain alert and creative while they imagine a day at work 10 years in the future. Once the group is quieted and relaxed, the facilitator reads the "Perfect Future Day Fantasy" script. The reading should be done slowly with expanded silent pauses provided throughout the script. When paced correctly, the script reading takes about 20 to 30 minutes to complete.

The guided imagery is followed by a period of discussion that is aimed at encouraging the girls to process their career fantasy. Suggested prompt questions to use in the discussion are provided in the appendix. Each participant is asked to recall her workday fantasy and to identify any of the primary values she listed on the *Rokeach Values Inventory* that surfaced during her fantasy. Throughout the discussion the counselor gently orchestrates the discussion to promote in depth exploration. Comments such as, "I noticed in your fantasy that you were able to enjoy your family life while holding the top leadership position in your company" or "You mentioned being a nurse. Did you know that many physicians have similar interests and goals?" are used by the facilitator in his/her efforts to reach the following objectives of the activity:

- **Career Exploration:** Listening to other's career dreams in a group setting naturally exposes girls to a variety of career opportunities they may not yet considered. Participants are free not only to dream and imagine about their own careers, they can collaborate in others' dreams as well.

- **Raising Aspirations:** Listening to girls talk about their dreams provides a natural and comfortable setting to gently nudge their aspirations toward more challenging and fulfilling career options. Doing so in a group setting validates and normalizes their talents and intellectual abilities and frees them to claim their talents and abilities and a source of pride and potential rather than as an embarrassment to hide. The pressure to dummy down evaporates as girls are allowed to dream big without the typical peer pressure to fit in with the crowd.

- **Incorporation of Values:** Teaching girls the importance of incorporating their values into their career dreams and plans begins by helping them identify, then apply, their values in their everyday activities. Deliberately pointing out how their values are surfaced in their fantasies provides them with a concrete example of how inseparable their values are from their interests, skills, and abilities. While their interests and skills may change, their values will remain the one constant across several different career choices.

- **Goal Setting:** The Future Day Fantasy provides a forum for discussion of barriers and dreams. Asking the girls how they plan to achieve their fantasized dreams and what barriers may encounter along the way sets in motion a concrete plan for them to follow. The insurmountable begins to shift to the possible.

- **Incorporation of Developmental and Career Theory:** The future day fantasy is an activity firmly rooted in theory. It provides a forum for mastery of many of the conflicts associated with adolescent development. It allows girls to experiment and try on different work and identity roles in a safe environment, to ponder temporal concepts of concrete present (what is) versus the imagined future (what can be); and to consolidate their growing sense of social responsibility and personal ideology by expressing their thoughts in a public setting. It also encourages them to engage in an activity, i.e., dreaming, that is a normal part of adolescent development. Cognitively, the future day fantasy activity provides a concrete and structured method to help girls advance from concrete operational thought toward formal operational thought. The intervention incorporates what we know from feminist theory about the importance of relationships to girls by creating a girl-friendly, cooperative, and companionable environment in which girls are liberated to explore and dream. Finally, use of the future day fantasy allows for cultural diversity. It is easily adaptable to varying cultural groups because the facilitator can present the exercise with sensitivity to cultural preferences. For example, a group of Native American girls for whom thoughts of the future maybe incongruent with their world-view can be guided through a "vision quest or journey" rather than "stepping into a time machine that will take them into the future."

The Values and Dreams of Bright Girls

So what can we learn from listening to girls' dreams and from attending to their values? To find out, the completed values inventories and future day fantasies transcriptions from 430 adolescent girls (average age of 15.42) who had attended the TARGETS career workshops at Arizona State University were examined. Several consistent themes emerged in the girls' fantasies. These included a sense of autonomy and leadership, a sense of pride and accomplishment, and an ability to balance high career aspirations with strong family values. The girls' values were evident in their imagined career day, with the majority of girls identifying "family security" and "self-respect" as either their first or second most strongly held value. Often the girls did not come from families where there was a sense of security and the girls wanted this in their adult lives. In addition, they realized that if they did not respect themselves, no one else would respect them. Also, self-respect meant taking care of themselves. This is a strong buffer against many of the at-risk behaviors of teenagers.

These values were followed by a "sense of freedom", "true friendship", and "spirituality." For many of these girls, religion or spirituality was an integral component of their lives and they visioned it as remaining a part of their future. Being girls, they of course wanted a future of loyal and faithful friends. Finally, part of the developmental process is evidenced in their desire for freedom and the ability to do what they wanted.

The girls frequently stated that they felt content, confident, and proud at the end of their workdays. They were often surprised at their detailed visualizations of their ability to lead others and/or own their own businesses. They pictured themselves enjoying the material rewards that paralleled their professional careers (e.g., business suits, big houses, luxury automobiles, and hired household help). The girls voiced surprise at the depth and detail of their thoughts and emotions during their fantasies.

Regardless of the content of their dreams or which value they identified, the girls expressed their excitement and understanding of the importance of incorporating their values into their career plans. They frequently expressed heightened self esteem and increased self-efficacy after giving voice to their dreams and having their values validated. Their comments lead us to believe that the addition of the future day fantasy activity and of values-exploration to traditional career counseling approaches will fill a void that too often strands our bright girls in a multi-potential trap. Yes, they can "be anything they want to be." Identifying personal value in their career endeavors may help fill the gap between their ability and their potential achievement.

5

Using the Vocational Preference Inventory with Talented At-risk Girls

Sandra M. Dannenbaum
Laura L. Huser
Sarah E. Lowery

What would you (as a teacher, a parent, or a counselor) say to an adolescent girl who you sense is working below her capabilities? You might see sparks of uncommon curiosity, notable leadership skills, or creative ability beyond that of her peers. Yet, you notice her drifting, getting into things she shouldn't, or becoming the classic underachiever. What would you tell her? How might you help? The following vignettes are an amalgam of the many talented at-risk girls seen in the TARGETS program. As we discuss the Vocational Preference Inventory, we will revisit these girls and their stories and share how the VPI can be used to seed transformation and open the door to possibilities...

Rosa is a 17-year old Hispanic female who is the youngest of six children in her family. She is a senior in high school whose grades have been slipping since the beginning of her sophomore year. As an elementary and junior high school student, Rosa's performance in school was above average. Now she ranks among the lowest in the class. Rosa has become increasingly quiet and her parents fear that the rumors about her being the leader of a local gang may be true. Rosa's teachers have tried to encourage her to work up to her potential but she does not see any value in working hard. She feels bitter and hopeless about school and has watched for years as her parents have been overworked and underpaid. Rosa is certain that she will end up the same way.

__Heather__ is a 16-year old White female who is a junior in high school. She has been on the honor role ever since her freshman year and is ranked 3rd in her class. She has always succeeded in every area in school from athletics to academics. After attending a seminar where she was exposed to universities across the country, Heather became aware that she could attend any school she desired. This was a huge dilemma for Heather; not only did she not know where she wanted to go to school, but also she had no idea what field in which to major. She consulted with the high school guidance counselor and he assured her that she could do anything that she wanted to because she was so bright. This did not help Heather at all; instead, the stress caused her to go the easy route, attend the local college and figure out her major along the way.

__Kim__ is a 17-year old African-American female who is oldest of three children in her middle-income family. She is a senior in high school and excels in all of her classes. She does especially well in her math and science classes and her teacher nominated her for a scholarship to study Chemistry at a well-known university. Kim *would be the first one in her family to pursue a college degree. When Kim obtained the scholarship, she was fearful that she would not succeed in college, let alone be able to major in Chemistry. When she went to her advisor at school with these fears, the advisor recommended that Kim not strive for such difficult goals but instead, attend a community college where she is guaranteed to do well. Kim is leaning toward pursuing a certification program to become a pharmacy technician because it will be much less stressful and the community college tuition will not be burdensome on her family. She can also save money by living at home.*

Impediments to career development:

For many young people, the development of occupational plans begins during late adolescence. For young women, this development may be impeded by many factors that include: a) a decrease in self-esteem, b) lack of exposure to possible careers, and c) lack of academic focus. While girls exhibit more advanced skills earlier in life than boys, one indicator of arrested development is the identification of fewer girls for gifted programs in junior high and high school (Silverman, 1986). This may be explained by a dramatic decrease in self-esteem for girls during their adolescent years (Gilligan, 1990).

McCormick and Wolf (1993) suggest that this drop in self-esteem may be related to the conflicting messages of adolescence regarding career aspirations and life goals. For example, a teenager might have dreams of being a scientist as well as being a mother. Since a career as a scientist may seem like a male domain, the girl may feel conflicting values – a desire to have a career that interests her, but also a desire to have a family. This may cause an adolescent to drop her advanced science class in favor of more feminine subject areas, or ones that will be more socially acceptable to her male counterparts. Girls often take less rigorous courses than do boys in high school. In fact, a study conducted by Kerr (1985) found that despite others' encouragement and recognition, young women have lower aspirations than do men by their senior year in high school.

Often, young women face a lack of exposure to the types of careers available to them. According to Super (1967), individuals between the ages of 14 and 18 first begin to crystallize vocational preferences. During the crystallization period, young people begin to form ideas about what work will be appropriate for them and start to create occupational self-concepts that will guide them in their choice of career. For young women, the teen years may be crucial. Adolescent girls make occupational plans within a contextual setting that deeply affects their chosen path. Influence of parents and peers, culture, lack of exposure to careers, and lack of role models profoundly influence the way in which they conceptualize their own career development.

Adolescents often adjust their career plans based on what they perceive of as "acceptable" for people of a particular social class, race/ethnicity, or gender (Steinberg, 1999). For young women, role models and exposure to a wide variety of careers during this period are crucial. Despite a shift away from sex-role stereotypes over the past 30 years, adolescent girls' vocational choices still tend to be concentrated in jobs that have traditionally been occupied by women (e.g., secretarial work, teaching, nursing) (Beutel & Marini, 1995). Conversely, fewer adolescent girls plan to enter jobs in which the thrust of work involves things (e.g., science and engineering) rather than people (Jozefowicz, Barber, Eccles, & Mollasis, 1994).

Finally, many of the adolescent girls seen at the TARGETS workshops have issues with "multi-potentiality." These girls have many interests but have not concentrated on one area. Often they are unable to focus and feel somewhat lost when they think about future careers. The danger of having too little focus lies in the possibility that they will just take the easiest route. When the easiest route is chosen, all of the barriers to reaching their highest potential become even more salient. These overwhelmed young women may be even more susceptible the pressures of sex-role stereotypes, pressures to underachieve, and negative cultural influences. The lack of female occupational role models or exposure to a variety of careers may then serve to perpetuate their decisions to settle for simplest route to a career or for no career at all.

Person-Environment Fit:

Research suggests that career selection and development is a complex interaction of three major domains: abilities, vocational interests, and personality characteristics (Kerr, 1994). Each of these domains uniquely influences career performance and must be viewed both separately and in conjunction with the other domains when helping others think about their careers. It has also been demonstrated that individual patterns within groups (i.e. engineers) will likely look more similar than will patterns of individuals between groups (i.e. engineers vs. nurses). A person who is an engineer is different in many important ways from a nurse or a teacher, even though intellectually they may be similar. Further, differences can also be seen between specialties within a given field. For example, a pediatrician and an oncologist or a math teacher and a gym teacher share the commonalities of their respective professions, but because of the differences between their jobs, they will also have distinctive differences in vocational interests and personality characteristics.

When encouraging at-risk girls to consider their life's work, it is important that teachers, counselors and parents consider (independently and collectively) these three domains (e.g., abilities, vocational interests, and personality characteristics) to increase the chance that those they help will be well matched with their occupations and with the organizations in which they work. The greater degree of similarity between a person's abilities, vocational interests, and personality and the job requirements, the higher the likelihood she will be vocationally satisfied, remain in her job, and be a productive employee. Therefore, this concept, often referred to as "person-environment fit," is important to keep in mind when contemplating vocational choices. In our workshops with TARGETS girls, the **Vocational Preference Inventory** (VPI; Holland, 1985) was used to assess vocational interests and to start the girls on their journey of career exploration. Following is an overview of the VPI and its utility with TARGETS girls.

The Vocational Preference Inventory:

The Vocational Preference Inventory was described by its author, John Holland, as "a personality-interest inventory composed entirely of occupational titles" (1985). While at face value, an occupational title approach may seem a little unusual, a closer look at Holland's theory and his model of personality types and occupational environments may yield a deeper understanding as to how occupational choices reflect individual personalities. Holland's typologies are only one way of examining career interests; however, not only is his theory popular around the world, it has amassed a wealth of significant empirical data. We chose the VPI for its strong theoretical foundation, overall clinical utility, economy, and brevity.

Briefly, the rationale that drives the VPI suggests that people's career interests reflect their motivations, skills, values, and knowledge (Holland, 1985). Over our lifetimes we develop stereotypes about different occupations and choose occupational interests based on our perceived views of these vocational stereotypes. Careers can imply status, intelligence, where we might fit in the community, things about our daily lives, and even our personalities. Holland theorized that there are six general personality types and that people resemble one type or some combination of two to three types. At the same time, Holland posited that work environments reflect these typologies and that people are attracted to environments where they may more frequently interact with others who share their approach to the world. The gist of Holland's theory is that the better people's personality types are reflected in their work environment and the more consistently the personal typologies match the work typologies, the better the person 'fits' her or his work environment and the more likely the person will be happy and successful in that work environment. This is referred to as Person-Environment Fit. The six general typologies (RIASEC) are: **1) Realistic, 2) Investigative, 3) Artistic, 4) Social, 5) Enterprising, and 6) Conventional.**
The Holland Typologies:

Holland presents his RIASEC model within a hexagonal frame. Starting in the upper left hand 'Realistic' corner (see Figure 1), the typologies follow one another clockwise. It is important to note that the closer one type is to another; the more the types have in common. Likewise, the farther apart they are, the fewer similarities.

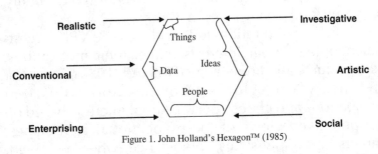

Figure 1. John Holland's Hexagon™ (1985)

For example, Conventional and Investigative types have more in common with Realistic types than they have with each other. Types directly opposite one another have the least in common. As you read about each one, the differences and similarities will become apparent.

Descriptions of the six Holland typologies:

· **Realistic** types tend to be attracted to 'hands on' occupations that require working with things rather than with people or ideas. People who like to work with tools and equipment, outdoors, or activities that lend themselves to physical prowess, mechanical ability, and concrete-type tasks often fall into the Realistic realm. Occupations in the skilled trades, i.e., construction, plumbing, electrician, and x-ray technician, are considered to be Realistic, as are agricultural and horticultural jobs, some military or police jobs, and athletics. Some engineering specialties are found in this realm. Pure Realistic types have become associated with certain values: tradition, common sense, and practicality. Because people who are Realistic spend a lot of their energy focused on working with things, they often view learning as a means to an end rather than a lifelong pursuit for understanding. In addition, Realistic types may struggle with interpersonal expression and may tend to favor direct action or words over diplomatic expression of thoughts and feelings (Holland, 1985; 1994).

· **Investigative** types live in the world of ideas and can fall in love with learning for its own sake. Inordinate curiosity, analytical ability, and abstract reasoning ability are attributes often found in Investigative types who are attracted to work environments where they can be independent and knowledge-seeking. Jobs in higher education, math, sciences, many engineering fields, as well as occupations that require analytical skills, professors at research universities, actuaries, and many medical professions are good fits for Investigative types. Individuals who score high in Investigative often do not feel a need to persuade or influence others to their way of thinking and often like to work alone where they are free to explore and discover new ideas and methodologies (Holland, 1985; 1994).

· **Artistic** types are also very independent people, and they share the world of ideas with Investigative types but through a different lens. Those who are most comfortable in the Artistic realm are drawn to beauty and cherish imagination and creativity through self-expression. As might be expected, people in the visual (e.g., painter, sculptor, clothes designer); literary (e.g., poet, novelist); dramatic (e.g., actor, performance artist); and musical arts (e.g., pianist, vocalist), fall into this category as well as those who are sensitive to, or deeply appreciative of, beauty in its many forms. Artistic types often chafe under a lot of structure and rules where they might feel their creativity and independence is stifled (Holland, 1985; 1994).

- **Social** types live in the world of people and are inspired by environments reflecting cooperation, generosity, and service to others. They tend to have a knack for working with people, are verbally adept, and are skilled listeners capable of showing understanding. They like to teach, explain things and to help others. Social types tend to be interested in people, enjoy working on teams, care about the welfare of others, and often serve their communities. Driven by their genuine caring and sense of community, they may seek to influence and persuade others. Social types are attracted to occupations such as social work, teaching, religious ministries, marriage and family counseling, psychology, school administration and other work environments that allow them to develop relationships with other people. They are often good at leading others, like to achieve, and are typically pleasant to be around (Holland, 1985; 1994).

- **Enterprising** types also like to influence and persuade others and share being people-oriented with Social types. Where Social types tend to use their people skills to help others. Enterprising people might be described as more status-seeking (i.e., prestige and/or financial gain). They enjoy using their abilities to persuade people to their point of view and are good at motivating and directing others. Salespeople, marketing and advertising professionals, politicians, small business owners, and corporate executives often score high in Enterprising. These occupations often involve interpersonal and/or financial risk-taking, competition, and status (Holland, 1985; 1994).

• **Conventional** types, the last in the RIASEC model, also enjoy status but not to the same degree as Enterprising types. People who score high in Conventional often value stability, efficiency, and accuracy and tend to do well in structured organizations where they know how they fit into the overall operations. Conventional types are often great record-keepers as they can be quite good at math, detail-oriented tasks, and data analysis: they live in the world of data. The world of data is similar to the world of things except in this case the "thing" is data, i.e., numbers, information, etc. Middle-managers, clerical workers, data base managers, accountants, and other administrative staff are occupations to which high scorers in the Conventional typology are attracted.

The VPI in TARGETS Workshops:

Using the VPI in TARGET workshops is useful in many ways and the results generated by completing the measure can provide valuable insight into how the TARGETS girls view themselves and their occupational choices. When reviewing the RIASEC hexagon during the one-on-one counseling session, counselors have an opportunity to explore where these girls are on their level of vocational maturity (familiarity with various jobs), their level of self-efficacy (belief that they can perform the job), and what their patterns of interests are compared to those of successful people in different occupations. The VPI helps to foster a better understanding of one's likes and dislikes and how these fit into different occupational worlds.

The VPI can also be useful as a tool to enhance current aspirations (e.g., doctor versus nurse) and to consider occupations that one was unaware existed (e.g., bioengineer). Let's consider Kim, one of our girls described at the beginning of this chapter.

The teacher who noticed Kim's aptitude for math and chemistry selected her for the TARGETS program. Kim seemed genuinely enthused in these challenging subjects. Kim scored very high in the Investigative (I) and Realistic (R) themes of Holland's RIASEC typologies, a two-letter code that, when considered with Kim's academic abilities, suggested a number of occupations far beyond entry-level medical service jobs with little room for the intellectual challenges Kim so loved. During the one-on-one session, her counselor was able to show Kim how the VPI captured her interests in medical service but also reflected her attraction to more challenging medical fields (ideas) as well as an interest in things. When Kim heard that she might consider being a psychiatrist or a biochemical engineer, she began to see a world far bigger and brighter as her career options expanded. She began to recognize that the challenging years at the university were just hoops to jump and not roadblocks. She now had more choices, more ideas, and more things to dream about.

This illustrates how the VPI can encourage young women to think about themselves in relation to the career world. In our work with TARGETS girls, this tool stimulates rich discourse about a girl's interests, where her interests lay within the RIASEC hexagon, as well as her hopes, dreams, barriers and fears that often accompany conversations about career decisions.

The following is a breakdown of the most frequently seen 2-letter codes for each racial/ethnic minority group that attended TARGETS workshops. As is evident, the workshops were enriched with young girls from diverse cultures. Even so, they shared much in common in respect to their vocational interests.

White Girls (n = 149)
1. Realistic/Investigative (n = 33; 22%)
(Possible careers: mechanical engineer, structural engineer, marine biologist, meteorologist, architect, astronautical engineer, geophysicist, archeologist)
2. Investigative/Artistic (n = 21; 14%)
(Possible careers: mystery writer, sociologist/ psychologist, investigative reporter; linguist, professor of literary studies, architect, computer animator)

Mexican American (n = 137)
1. Realistic/Investigative (n = 22; 16%)
(Possible careers: mechanical engineer, structural engineer, marine biologist, meteorologist, architect, astronautical engineer, geophysicist, archeologist)
2. Realistic/Conventional (n = 17; 12%)
(Possible careers: electrician, military officer, math professor, database manager, accountant, statistician, business manager)

Native American (n = 108)
1. Realistic/Investigative (n = 32; 30%)
(Possible careers: mechanical engineer, structural engineer, marine biologist, meteorologist, architect, astronautical engineer, geophysicist, archeologist
2. Conventional/Realistic (n = 22; 20%)
(Possible careers: electrician, military officer, math professor, database manager, accountant, statistician, business manager)

African American (n = 48)
1. Realistic/Investigative (n = 9; 19%)
(Possible careers: mechanical engineer, structural engineer, marine biologist, meteorologist, architect, astronautical engineer, geophysicist, archeologist)
2. Conventional/Enterprising (n = 9;   19%)
(Possible careers: bank president, investments manager, small business owner, international business manager; global account specialist, employment lawyer, finance manager)

Asian American (n = 21)
1. Realistic/Investigative (n = 8; 38%)
(Possible careers: mechanical engineer, structural engineer, marine biologist, meteorologist, architect, astronautical engineer, geophysicist, archeologist)

Other similarities across cultures observed in the workshops were the presence of elevated and flat profiles. An elevated profile simply means that the scores on several themes are equally elevated above the average range of scores. This elevation of scores is often indicative of a young woman who is interested in many occupations. Talented girls are usually good at many things, and a challenging task is getting them to narrow their field of choices. When a profile is equally elevated across many themes in the RIASEC model, it may simply mean that there is no consistent occupational orientation and the girl would be equally comfortable in any of several working environments.

In order to explore this possibility, identifying where one fits within the hexagon can be a valuable exercise. An important part of the TARGETS counseling session is the reading of the RIASEC descriptors and inquiring which descriptions fit the girl best. Evidence as to why the description fits can be given by way of real-life examples. In many cases this form of self-exploration often reveals that by having an interest in a particular subject matter involved in an occupation (i.e. liking math) does not necessarily mean that one shares similar interests with people in that occupation (math teacher). As a result, if a career were chosen based solely on the preference for math, the day-to-day life of working as a math teacher would probably not be enjoyed.

Remember **Heather** of too many choices? Heather was bright and successful in all her endeavors. Third in her class, she was able to meet the rigors of many subject areas. She could write her ticket to any university, but in what field should she focus her efforts? Heather's VPI profile was elevated on all RIASEC codes. In the counseling session, the counselor asked Heather to imagine herself doing the various jobs for six months or longer. Would she still enjoy each occupation? "Imagine," the counselor asked, "if you were a dentist, would you enjoy looking at people's teeth day in and day out?" Heather soon realized that while many jobs sounded attractive, important, prestigious, etc., she actually had little knowledge about the nature of many of the occupations. The counselor talked about exploring various occupations on the Internet, and focused on the wealth of information available in the *Occupational Outlook Handbook*. Using the information they discovered when talking about Heather's VPI profile, they set immediate goals for Heather to gather information about various jobs. They set a second goal for Heather to interview some people in occupations of interest after she narrowed down her options. Heather was able develop concrete actions she could take to resolve her career dilemma.

Another common occurrence seen with TARGET girls is what is known as "a flat profile". This means that the test-taker scored low on all six themes, and no elevation was revealed on any one theme. Some of the reasons for a flat profile include not being familiar with a variety of occupations, not understanding what the job entails, low self-efficacy (thinking they are not smart enough, or that it is a guy's job), lack of belief that it is possible to attain (requires too much schooling, money, time, etc.), and/ or denying being gifted. An important consideration to keep in mind is that many young people have limited experience with the working world and the careers that are available to them. This is often true in lower SES groups where exposure to a wide range of careers is limited as are resources to achieve career goals. Finally, many girls may feel obligated to their families and loved ones not to leave for extended periods of time for schooling or training. If they do leave, they are often expected to pick a vocation that will benefit the family and/or tribe of origin. Any one or a combination of these reasons could conceivably cause a TARGETS girl to have a flat profile. A flat profile may also be indicative of depressed mood, loss of hope, or an inability to envision the future. Counselors and parents need to look for other signs of depression or hopelessness including suicidal thoughts.

Unfortunately, we saw **Rosa**'s story too often repeated in our TARGETS workshops. Rosa had lots of potential. The motivation to achieve that she'd exhibited in elementary and junior high school was still there, and now manifested in her ability to lead her gang. She had seen too many friends die. Rosa saw little hope and very few options. Rosa was pretty "checked out" when she came to the TARGETS sessions. The other girls watched her closely and cloned her behavior. During the assessment phase, each girl was asked to focus on her own materials. Rosa went through the motions of responding to the items on the VPI. When scored, her profile was flat with just a slight elevation on Enterprising. In the counseling session she was unenthusiastic, to say the least. The counselor introduced the VPI results and talked about how a profile like Rosa's sometimes meant that the person was feeling really depressed and without much hope. The counselor asked if Rosa had ever felt that way. Rosa sat quietly as tears ran down her cheeks. The counselor sat with her allowing the feelings to be present and giving Rosa the time she needed. Rosa shared her grief at the recent loss of a childhood friend and talked about how she had seen too many in her neighborhood die. She talked about feeling like she too would die very soon. The counselor asked Rosa if there was anything in which she found joy. She responded that she felt joy in being the leader of her gang, and how being a leader made her feel important. The counselor was able to encourage this spark and toward the end shared briefly how Rosa might use her leadership abilities to improve her neighborhood. This session did not follow the prescribed TARGETS protocol as the emotional content of the session and its importance took precedence over research procedures. The counselor followed up with the TARGETS program administrators who contacted Rosa's school counselor. The school counselor worked to link Rosa to available mental health services.

As discussed earlier, elevated profiles may be indicative of multiple potentiality or undefined interests. Flat and elevated profiles often indicate a high need for additional information about occupations and vocational opportunities. In flat profiles, respondents may deselect occupations because they have negative stereotypes about them. The opposite is true with those with elevated profiles. In either case, developing avenues where girls can get needed information about the world of work is an integral part of the TARGETS workshops.

The VPI is a practical tool in helping TARGETS counselors highlight interests expressed by the young women. The six-point hexagon provides a quick and easy way to help the girls see how their interests relate to real-world jobs. This measure therefore provides them with a useful framework to begin the formation and pursuit of satisfying career goals.

Each of the adolescent girls presented in the vignettes at the beginning of this chapter represents a possible TARGETS participant. All of the girls are dealing with complicated issues such as low self-esteem, low educational self-efficacy, multipotentiality, and lack of female career role models. These factors are all embedded within the context of race, socio-economic status, and dominant cultural frame. As young women "at-risk" they are faced with the very real possibility that they may not achieve their potential. The TARGETS workshops attempt to ensure that girls such as these have the opportunity to gain the necessary exposure to support systems and role models that will inspire them to achieve their goals and dreams. Finally, the VPI helps TARGETS counselors in working with girls to uncover and understand their interests within the context of a wide range of career possibilities. This process in the TARGETS workshop provides an integral step toward vocational self-discovery and fulfillment.

Using the VPI in your own workshops:

At first sight, the VPI is not an impressive instrument. It is, after all, a list of one hundred sixty vocational titles beside which the test-taker checks whether or not she likes or dislikes that particular job. That's it. In psychology lingo, it lacks what we call "face validity". Still, the VPI is considered by many professionals to be a highly reliable instrument and is widely used. It takes approximately thirty minutes to complete and can be hand-scored in three to five minutes. Many adolescents, especially those with little exposure to the world of work, have limited knowledge about the occupations listed. There are often many questions about what one does in a specific job, or what it is. "What's a truck farmer?" was an often heard phrase. When using this instrument with adolescents, it is useful to look over the VPI in advance and be prepared with brief descriptions of those occupations you suspect your test taker(s) might be unfamiliar.

Some of our TARGETS workshop cohorts were comprised of highly resistant girls who showed little interest in completing the various assessment tools that were integral to the TARGETS process. Like Rosa, there are many at-risk girls facing daily life-changing events. They often struggle to see the utility of checking off job likes and dislikes. Building rapport early-on in the workshop, prior to the assessment process, is very helpful in ensuring usable test profiles. Being excited and encouraging about the process, having a brief and understandable explanation of what will be learned by their active participation, and being there to provide brief and accurate answers to their questions will help the assessment part of the workshop go smoothly.

Counselor training on the VPI was an integrated component of the TARGETS model. In the counseling phase of the workshop, having counselors trained and familiar with the instrument ensures quality interpretations. Counselors should have an understanding of the various types of profiles, the specific challenges of each type, and knowledge of effective interventions to meet these challenges.

References:

Beutel, A., & Marini, M. (1995). Gender and values. *American Sociological Review, 60,* 436-448.

Gilligan, C. (1990). Teaching Shakespeare's sister: Notes from the underground of female adolescence. In Gilligan, Lyons & Hanmer (Eds.). *Making connections: The relational wolds of adolescent girls at Emma Willard School.* Cambridge, MA. Harvard University Press.

Holland, J. (1985). *The Vocational Preference Inventory (VPI).* Odessa, FL: Psychological Assessment Resources, Inc.

Holland, J. (1994). *The Self Directed Search (SDS).* Odessa, FL: Psychological Assessment Resources, Inc.

Jozefowicz, D., Barber, B., Eccles, J., & Mollasis, C. (1994). *Relationships between maternal and adolescent values and beliefs: Gender difference and implications for occupational choice.* Paper presented at the biennial meeting for the Society for Research on Adolescence, San Diego.

Kerr, B. (1994). *Smart Girls (Revised Edition).* Gifted Psychology Press: Scottsdale, AZ.

McCormick, M. E., & Wolf, J. S. (1993). *Intervention programs for gifted girls. Roeper Review, 16,* 85-87.

Silverman, L. (1986). *What happens to the gifted girl?* In C. J. Maker (Ed.) Critical issues in gifted education (pp. 43-90). Rockville, MD: Aspen Publishers, Inc.

Steinberg, L. (1999). *Adolescence.* Boston: McGraw-Hill

Super, D. (1967). *The psychology of careers.* New York: Harper & Row.

6

Personality Assessment Using the Personality Research Form

Barbara Kerr
Margaret Corrigan

Lisa *is an attractive, easygoing teenager.*

Her friends describe her as a born leader with a witty sense of humor. She likes to compete, be in charge and to persuade others. She is intelligent and independent yet she thinks and acts "on the spur of the moment." She has poor work habits in that she dislikes routine, gives up easily and gets off track in favor of silly, fun experiences.

Is there a personality "type" associated with talented but at risk girls? What personality traits might these girls have in common? Is there more than one personality profile associated with talented at risk girls? The answers to these questions are beginning to emerge in the research of the TARGETS program. The TARGETS program, throughout its history, has used the Personality Research Form, based on Murray's theory of personality. Murray was a founding member of the Boston Psychoanalytic Society. In studying an individual's life, Murray's strategy consists of reducing the complexities of behavior to identifiable and manageable structural units. Murray identified and developed a Needs-Press model of interaction in which personal needs, or "motivational personality characteristics," represent the tendency for individuals to move in the direction of goals, whereas the environmental press is the external situational counterpart that either supports or frustrates the expression of these needs (Aldridge & Fraser, 1997). Murray's motivational concepts are considered to be his most important contributions to psychological theory. These concepts are need, press, thema, and unity-thema. For our purposes, we will only address need and press.

A need stands for a force in the mind. It organizes and directs perception, memory, thought, and action in such a way as to reduce dissatisfaction and increase satisfaction. Needs may be aroused by internal states, such as hunger, or they may be set in action by external stimulation, such as the sight of food. A press helps or hinders the efforts of an individual to reach a desired goal. Typical presses are poverty, illness, loss, en-couragement, and help.

This personality theory was particularly suitable to understanding the characteristics of the talented at risk girls and translating these characteristics into ideas that they could readily understand and apply to their own lives.

The Personality Research Form, Version E (PFR-E; (Jackson, 1989) was used to make personality assessments. The PRF-E is made up of 352 self-descriptive true-false statements developed to represent 22 distinct personality needs. These personality needs include: Abasement, Achievement, Affiliation, Aggression, Autonomy, Change, Cognitive Structure, Defendence, Dominance,

Endurance, Exhibition, Harmavoidance, Implusivity, Nurturance, Order, Play, Sentience, Social Recognition, Succorance, and Understanding. The PRF was originally developed to measure Murray's personality characteristics and is currently used to assess normal areas of personality functioning in nonclinical samples. Version E is specifically designed for use with adolescents. Internal consistencies for these scales range from .54 to .85 (Jackson). Construct validities for these scales range from .36 to.74 (Jackson,1989). Measures of convergent and discriminant validities indicate associations with other personality measures and disassociations with dissimilar types

The data for all PRF administered to TARGETS girls were analyzed in order to determine which needs were the most prevalent among this population. Robinson-Kurpius & Kerr (2001) have reported that talented girls do have in common certain personality characteristics. In their research spanning nearly a decade, Robinson-Kurpius & Kerr have found that talented, at-risk girls experience lowered needs for achievement coupled with a lowered need to avoid harm. These girls also have higher needs for play, exhibitionism, aggression, impulsiveness, defendence (i.e., need to be highly defended) and need for peer affiliation. For the girls who completed the PRF ($n = 490$), . Although no T-score was more than one standard deviation greater or less than the mean of 50, characteristics indicative of an at-risk profile were evident. Mean scores were elevated for Play ($M = 54.39$, $SD = 9.66$), Impulsivity ($M = 52.20$, $SD = 8.72$), Defendence ($M = 55.59$, $SD = 9.79$), Aggression ($M = 54.33$, $SD = 9.71$), Affiliation ($M = 54.06$, $SD = 7.93$), and Exhibition ($M = 53.01$, $SD = 8.98$). Mean scores were depressed for Harmavoidance ($M = 47.62$, $SD = 9.70$) and Achievement ($M = 9.70$) and Achievement

($\underline{M} = 47.38$, $\underline{SD} = 9.73$).

These girls represent a sample that could accurately be described as at-risk due to personality characteristics. They have a low need to avoid harm and for achievement while they are highly defended, tend to be aggressive and impulsive, like to play and to be the center of attention (exhibition), and need affiliation with their peers. These personality characteristics were confirmed in the girls' self report of their beliefs and behaviors. The following sections describe these characteristic needs of talented at risk girls, and then particular combinations are addressed.

The need for Defendence was one of the highest scale scores for talented at risk girls. Defendence is the need to defend oneself from real or imagined harm. Most talented at risk girls have had experiences that made them feel vulnerable. Frequently, they had found it necessary to develop a set of skills for defending themselves verbally in the classroom and at home. Sometimes, they developed a mask of indifference or toughness. Sometimes, they created a role of a pleasing, smiling girl while maintaining a wariness. In addition, many of the girls were ironic in their conversation and cutting when criticized by their peers.

That defendence is a high score for these girls is interesting in the light of findings by Kerr (1997) that most eminent women had "thorns" and "shells." That is, those with thorns had a sharp or sarcastic sense of humor; they argued intensely for their point of view; or they were quick to be confrontive or angry when attacked by others. Those with "shells" were shy, introverted, or sometimes even seemed emotionless. It may be that the development of defendence is important for women who are pioneers in occupations that are traditionally male dominated; in addition, women scholars, artists, and scientists are frequently called upon to defend their work and their ideas with passion and assertiveness. Therefore, in counseling talented at risk girls, we were careful to warn of the dangers of being too suspicious, particularly of those who were in teaching and mentoring roles. However, we also reassured them that defendence was often an important component of resilience and the capacity to survive against tough odds.

We interpreted high scores in aggression similarly, showing how the characteristic of arguing for one's point of view and asserting one's rights requires a need for aggression. We were careful to point out that on this personality test, aggression does not mean a tendency for violence, but rather a tendency to be bold and even brash, as well as assertive. The girls were helped to discuss situations in which the need for aggression could get them into trouble, and the ways in which they could channel the need for aggression into sports and academic competition.

The need for play was another high score for these girls. Because this is a test normally taken by young adults, it makes sense that adolescents would score higher on play. However, when girls talked about their lives, it became clear that this group really did feel a need for more play in their lives – not because they were by nature more frivolous than other girls, but because so many of them had been deprived of the opportunity for recreation, relaxation, and fun. Many girls worked as well as went to school, some of them in arduous positions. Most of the employed girls were employed in fast food settings or babysitting, both occupations that required constant attention and little opportunity for socializing with other adolescents. In addition, many of the girls had responsibilities for siblings, and even occasionally for the care of their mothers or fathers who might be ill or troubled by addiction. Therefore, it became clear to us that the need for play was elevated precisely because these girls longed for more fun and less hardship.

Another high score was Affiliation. These girls also hungered for the pleasure of being with friends, of being liked and valued by peers, and of sharing their deepest feelings with a good friend. Like most teenage girls, they loved friendship and romance, and hoped to find more time in their lives for both. In the groups, it also became clear that despite their high scores on defendence, the girls were able to trust and like their counselors and the other girls when it became clear that it was a friendly, warm environment. We helped girls to see how high scores on affiliation could help them to find and sustain their social support system. We also made the connection between high scores on affiliation and success in occupations that involved group activities, caring, and friendliness. For those with interests in science and engineering, we stressed how useful these characteristics were in occupations that needed "people friendly people."

Low scores included achievement and harm avoidance. It is interesting that a group of girls who had actual high achievements in math and science scored low in the need for achievement. In counseling sessions, we learned that girls who scored below the mean in the need for achievement were often girls who resisted the competitiveness that was associated with this need. Many of the Native American girls felt strongly that achievement should be personal rather than public, and did not like the items linked to concerns about "being the best." We talked seriously with girls about the need to be motivated toward achievement of their goals even when not wanting to act competitively. We talked about the intrinsic versus extrinsic achievement motivation, and many of the lower scoring girls talked about wanting to achieve their own goals rather than somebody else's. Some of the girls had gotten failing grades in courses where they disliked the teacher or the methods; counselors pointed out that this merely hurt the girl, not the teacher, and the girls often laughingly agreed.

Finally, low scores on Harmavoidance did cause us deep concern. Low scores on Harmavoidance mean a tendency to take physical risks. Physical risks might include such teen behaviors as riding on a motorcycle without a helmet, getting drunk, and engaging in unsafe sex. Some of the girls were clearly thrill-seekers, enjoying any kind of adventure; we were sure to reinforce adventurousness while cautioning them against extreme risks. Low harmavoidance, is after all, also a measure of fearlessness; for many of these girls, this characteristic would indeed be required to overcome the barriers they perceived in their environments – particularly those who suffered from physical abuse and physical hardship.

In addition to the specific scale scores, we attempted to understand particular and frequently observed combinations. These clusters of characteristics formed profiles that we identified as "red flag profiles." "Homemaker," "Bad Girl," "Bungee Jumper," and the "Artiste" are four common personality profiles that emerge in talented girls.

The **"Homemaker"** represents a girl who is Conventional, with high needs for nurturance, succorance, and affiliation and low need for autonomy. Girls with this profile tend to have low self-esteem and want to be taken care of (i.e., "a female wants to be taken care of by a male" and "School is scary! I have to find a boyfriend!"). This girl can be encouraged towards other "Conventional" areas (e.g., accounting, bookkeeping) or may want to consider being a veterinarian, teacher of small children, or physical therapist. For most of these girls, homemaker is not their first career choice, but their lack of confidence and difficulty choosing a direction is heading them that way.

The **"Bad Girl"** profile is a combination of high defendence, aggression, and exhibition. She is non-conforming, is involved in gang-type-activity, and difficult to talk to. With high defendence, these girls may have had some kind of physical, emotional, or sexual abuse, either currently or in their history. These girls are more likely to be vigilant and aggressive -they are always willing to "fight back". These girls may have great promise in acting and in athletics, where their assertiveness and desire to be the center of attention is fulfilled.

The **"Bungee Jumper"** tends to be a combination of high need for impulsivity and play, with low need for harm-avoidance. This girl may be in danger of hurting herself with high physical risk activities, because she lacks the judgment to make good decisions about her well being. She may also mistake a dangerous situation for a playful or fun situation. Girls with this profile can convert their energy into creativity, courage and spontaneity (e.g., outward bound, outdoor activities); with a well structured and intense training program, they can do well in military leadership positions.

Finally, the **"Artiste"** profile, which is a combination of low endurance, high change, and high impulsivity. Therefore, although creative, they may not have well-developed study skills. These girls may be praised for their spontaneity and creative approach, while being warned about the need to learn the tools of their trade, and to persist despite fatigue and encouragement.

Challenges in assessing adolescent personality:

Giftedness and talent are not the same. Giftedness refers to ability whereas talent usually refers to competence in one or more areas of performance. "Individuals who are gifted may not necessarily be talented. Motivation is a catalyst in transforming giftedness to talent. Two common subgroups of gifted children who are difficult to identify are a) gifted underachievers, and b) gifted children who are culturally different. Both types may appear either disruptive or passive to teachers, educators and counselors.

A second confounding component in assessing personality is creativity. Creative girls are more readily distinguished by their interests, attitudes and personality traits than by intellectual abilities, because creativity and intelligence are only moderately overlapping (Kerr& Gagliardi,2002). Without the need for autonomy, persistence, and impulsivity, creativity cannot flourish, no matter how much intelligence the young person might possess. However, these characteristics may make a girl seem difficult and unpredictable to teachers. Helson (1985) captured this dilemma in the following quotation:

"Young people with creative potential have complex and contradictory aspects of personality. They have high aspirations, originality, independence, idealism and emotional investment in symbolic activity. They may also have precarious self-esteem, need for support, fear of intimacy, stubbornness, rebelliousness, and self-preoccupation. Some of these characteristics contribute to creative productivity, but others may lead to vacillation, failure, or redirection of goals.

As young people move from one life-situation to another, new demands arise, and the outcome of events at one stage changes the person's ability to meet the problems of the next. ... "Social and economic factors influence the actualization of creative careers in large segments of society and among minority or low-caste groups." (Helson, 1985, p.150)

How Murray's Needs/Press theory & the PRF is useful for at risk girls:

Murray's theory and the use of the PRF are particularly helpful in describing and assisting talented at risk girls for the following reasons. First of all, although the reading level is high, presenting a challenge to English learners, the conceptual level of the PRF is excellent for these bright girls. The idea of "needs" seem more appealing to girls as personality descriptors than traits and they like the sophistication of the labels that are used for each need. The fact that a need can motivate a girl toward a negative or a positive goal is important to providing a nonjudgmental assessment, for counselors can present both sides of these tendencies. Also, the instrument must be interpreted as a "snapshot" of current needs. Although a few scales have stability over the course of a lifetime, most of them are subject to fluctuations as a result of hunger and satiety for particular experiences.

Therefore, this instrument seems to be both a powerful and appropriate instrument for assessing the personalities of gifted girls. With skilled interpretation, the PRF can help girls to see how their needs compare to others and how their patterns of needs suit them to particular environments, relationships, and work. It can increase confidence and self esteem when counselors show how positive, socially constructive behaviors can emerge from needs. Finally, this rich instrument helps talented girls and women to understand on a profound level the complexity and uniqueness of the gifts they have to give the world.

References:

Aldridge, J. M. and Fraser, B. J. (1997). Examining science classroom environments in a cross national study. *Proceedings Western Australian Institute for Educational Research Forum 1997.* http://cleo.murdoch.edu.au/waier/forums/1997/aldridge.html

Helson, R. (1985). Which of those young women with creative potential became productive? Personality in college and characteristics of parents. *Perspective in Personality, 2,* 49-80.

Jackson, D. N. (1989). *Personality Research Form—Form E. Manuel.* Port Huron, MI: SigmaAssessment Systems

Kerr, B. A. & Gagliardi, C. (2002). Measuring creativity. In Davis, S. Handbook of positive psychology assessment. London, England: Pergamon.

Murray, H. A. (1938). *Explorations in Personality.* New York: Oxford University Press.

Robinson Kurpius, S. E., & Kerr, B. A. (2001). *Guiding girls into engineering math and science.* Paper presented at the American Educational Research Association Annual Meeting, Seattle, WA.

Shulman, L. (1992). Towards a pedagogy of cases. In J. H. Shulman (Ed.), *Case Methods in Teacher Education.* New York: Teachers College Press.

Tobin, K. & Fraser, B. J. (1997). Qualitative and quantitative landscapes of classroom learning environments. In B. J. Fraser and K. G. Tobin (Eds.) *The International Handbook of Science Education.* Dordrecht, The Netherlands: Kluwer Academic Publishers.

Walberg, H. J., Fraser B. J. & Welch, W. W. (1986). A test of a model of educational productivity among senior high school students. *Journal Educational Research, 79,* 133-139.

Walberg, H. J., Pascarella, E., Haertel, G. D., Junker, L. &
     Boulanger, F. D. (1981). Probing a model of
     educational productivity with National Assessment
     samples of early adolescents. *American
     Psychologist, 62,217-256.*
Wallace, J. & Chou, C. Y. (1997). *Sociocultural influences
     on the classroom learning environment.* Paper
     presented at the Annual Meeting of the National
     Association for Research into Science Teaching,
     Chicago.

Section 3

Impact of TARGETS and GEOS: Research Findings

It is very important to evaluate the effectiveness of any program. Therefore, two comprehensive evaluation studies of the TARGETS/GEMS and the GEOS programs were conducted. In addition, a long-term follow-up, qualitative study was conducted of the GOES program. While the TARGETS intervention had the most powerful impact on its participants, GEOS was able to influence the educational self-efficacy of the talented college freshman women and served a role in keeping them in their STEM career dreams. The value of GEOS and its impact of the lives of these young women was highlighted in the qualitative study.

7

The Impact of TARGETS on Adolescent Girls' Self-Beliefs and Behaviors

Sharon E. Robinson Kurpius
Barbara A. Kerr

In 1992, Drs. Kerr and Robinson Kurpius combined their two interests, working with the gifted student and helping the at-risk student, to create an intervention, called the Talented At-Risk Girls: Encouragement and Training for Sophomores project (TARGETS). The goal of TARGETS was to enhance the career development of minority and low-income girls who had strong academic potential in math and science. This intervention incorporated activities found to be effective in encouraging identification with and leadership in math science careers as well as activities specifically devised for this project based on theory and research on self-esteem and self-efficacy. The guidance laboratory approach that forms the basis of the workshop has been found to raise gifted girls' career aspirations (Kerr, 1981) and to increase sense of purpose and career identity (Kerr & Erb, 1992). A "girl-friendly" environment based on research in science education was created in which the girls, selected by their schools, met counselors and women scientists who discussed their own career development and gave the girls specific encouragement toward their goals. Mentors who would be available to the girls throughout high school and into college were provided; the counselors who worked with the girls pledged to continue to correspond with the girls as long as they perceived it to be useful.

The TARGETS Girls

Girls were nominated by school counselors or math/science teachers, who were directed to select girls with high grades in math and science who seemed to be at risk for not achieving their career goals. Risk factors might include low self-esteem and self-efficacy related to school, poverty, unsafe behaviors, or poor family support for goals. After permission was granted by a girl's parents or guardian, she became eligible to participate in TARGETS.

Over this seven-year time period, 502 girls, ranging in age from 11 to 20 ($M = 15.46$, $SD = 1.14$), received the TARGETS program. The girls represented 45 different high schools from all areas of Arizona (rural, urban, suburban, and reservation). The majority were in 10th grade ($n = 257$, 33.2%); although grade level varied from 6th grade ($n = 4$, .8%) to 12th grade ($n = 23$, 4.8%). Of those who identified ethnicity, 166 (33.2%) were Caucasian, 134 (26.8%) Hispanic, 112 (22.4%), Native American, 55 (11%) African American, 21 (4.2%) Asian American, and 12 (4.8%) "other."

Reports of family constellation revealed that 245 (49.5%) were from intact families, 152 (30.7%) from mother-only families, 76 (15.4%) from stepfamilies, and 22 (4.4%) from father-only families. Information on parental education and employment indicated that the majority ($\underline{n}$ = 257, 59.6%) of fathers had graduated from high school (or had a GED), had attended some college or technical school, or held a two-year degree and that 390 (84.6%) of the fathers were employed. For mothers, 301 (64.7%) had graduated from high school (or had a GED), had attended some college, or held a two-year degree and 376 (76%) were employed. Of these, 191 (42.5%) were in traditional female jobs/careers, while 146 (32.5%) were in nontraditional jobs/careers.

The Intervention: TARGETS

Although begun in late 1992, TARGETS was initially funded by the National Science Foundation (NSF) in 1994. The purpose of the program is to provide a values-based career intervention to mathematically and scientifically talented girls who are at risk for not achieving their career dreams. A full-day program, TARGETS was implemented across seven years. Components of the program include introductions using a values inventory, assessment of self beliefs (self esteem and educational self efficacy), a guided imagery exercise focusing on a perfect work day 10 years in the future, completion and individual interpretation of a career interest inventory and a personality test, a group discussion of barriers (at-risk behaviors) to career attainment, assessments of self-beliefs, and goal setting.

A three-year extension of the TARGETS program, Guiding Girls into Engineering, Math, and Science (GEMS), was funded by NSF in 1997. Under the auspice of this grant, TARGETS was continued and a component designed to teach school personnel (teachers, counselors, and administrators) and professors about the TARGETS program was added.

An Evaluation of the Effectiveness of TARGETS

This study utilized a within subjects design to evaluate the impact of the TARGETS program on the career behaviors, self-beliefs, and at-risk behaviors of teenage girls. During the first two years of the TARGETS program, in addition to the pre-assessment, 131 girls were retested immediately following their involvement in TARGETS. For the following five years, girls were pretested at the start of the TARGETS day and then were assessed again (first followed up; $n = 183$) at their home schools approximately three to four months after their involvement in TARGETS. In the fall of 2001, a long-term second follow-up survey was sent to all girls for whom there was a home address ($n = 180$). Of these, 34 were returned with no forwarding address and 97 were completed and returned.

Instruments Used in TARGETS

In addition to a demographic sheet, girls completed the Rosenberg Self Esteem scale (Rosenberg, 1965), the Educational Self Efficacy—Adolescents scale (Robinson, 1992b), the Career Behaviors Inventory, and the Adolescent At-Risk Behaviors Inventory (Robinson, 1992a). Two standardized measures, the Personality Research Form (Jackson, 1984) and the Vocational Preference Inventory, as well as the Rokeach Values (Rokeach, 1967) Inventory, were completed for use in the individual career guidance counseling session.

Demographic Information. Each girl answered questions about her age, grade, self-identified ethnicity, school activities, family members, educational level attained by parents, parental employment, religious affiliation, whether she was employed, completed math and science courses, and career goals and perceived obstacles. The long-term follow-up questionnaire presented questions about high school graduation date and grade point average (GPA), marital status, age, what they were currently doing (school and work), courses taken in math, science, and technology, and perceived obstacles to attaining their career dream.

Career Aspirations. The Career Exploration Activity Inventory developed for the TARGETS program was utilized to assess career behaviors and career aspirations. Girls indicated whether they had talked to 11 different individuals (e.g., parents, teachers, counselors) about careers in the last two months. Scores could range from zero to 11, with higher scores reflecting more career-related behavior. The Cronbach alpha for the items in this scale was .67 for the pretest and .67 for the first follow-up. Girls were also asked to list what careers they have thought about pursuing. The first career listed was coded for level of required education and was used as a measure of career aspiration. The *Occupational Outlook Handbook* (1996) was consulted to match career goal with education required.

Self–Esteem. The Rosenberg Self-Esteem Scale (SES, Rosenberg, 1965) measures one's feelings of self worth and was specifically designed for high school students (Fischer & Corcoran, 1994). A sample item is "At times I think that I am no good at all." Scores can range from 10 to 40, with higher scores indicating higher self-esteem. For the 502 girls at pretest, the Cronbach alpha was .84. For the 131 girls at post-test, the alpha coefficient was .87. At the first and second follow-up, it was .83.

Educational Self-Efficacy-Adolescence (ESEA). Developed by Robinson (1992b), the ESEA measures an individual's confidence in being able to accomplish various education related tasks. Participants rate themselves on a 7-point Likert scale from Not Sure to Very Sure they can complete a task. The ESEA is comprised of four subscales: (1) Job Self-Efficacy assesses efficacy for completing education/training for 30 different occupations; (2) School Self-Efficacy assesses belief in one's ability to do well in 13 basic high school courses. This scale was further divided in order to specifically examine math-science school efficacy: (3) Grade Self-Efficacy is belief that one can get an A or B in eight school subjects. It was also subdivided so that grade efficacy in math-science could be examined; and (4) Future Self-Efficacy, consisting of 21 items, assesses one's feelings about statements about the future. Items within each subscale are summed and divided by the number of items to produce scores that can range from one to seven.

Internal consistency reliabilities for these four scales for the TARGETS girls at pretest were .96 for Job Self-Efficacy, .93 for School Self-Efficacy, .92 for math-science school efficacy, .90 for Grade Self-Efficacy, .85 for math-science grade efficacy, and .77 for Future Self-Efficacy. These reliability coefficients were stable across the post-test and the first follow-up, varying no more than .02.

Adolescent At-Risk Behaviors Inventory (AARBI). This inventory was developed specifically for the TARGETS program (Robinson, 1992a) and has been modified as needed. The original 27-item survey yielded seven subscales—Driving/Safety, Exercise, Cigarette Use, Sexual Behavior, Alcohol Use, Drug Use, and Suicide. The current version, which added items related to gang involvement and body image, is comprised of seven subscales: Exercise (3 items, alpha = .68); Cigarette Use (4 items, alpha = .77); Sexual Behaviors (4 items, alpha = .85); Substance Use (6 items combining alcohol and drug use, alpha = .79), Suicidality (4 items, alpha = .84), Gang Involvement

(5 items, alpha = .87), and Body Image (2 times, alpha = .79). These alpha coefficients remained relatively stable across time. Responses within each subscale are summed with higher scores reflecting more at-risk behaviors for each scale except for exercise. For exercise a lower score indicated less participation in activities defined as exercise.

Our Findings and What They Mean for Working with Talented At-Risk Girls

Four global research questions were posed. The first asked about the characteristics of talented, at-risk teenage girls. The next three asked about career related behaviors, self-beliefs, and at-risk behaviors.

Characteristics of Talented At-Risk Teenage Girls

Values. The girls were asked to rank their top three values out of the 20 values presented on the Rokeach Values Inventory. The values that received the most frequent endorsements (summing across first, second, and third rankings) were Family Security ($f = 213$), Self Respect ($f = 153$), True Friendship ($f = 138$), Freedom ($f = 120$), and Health ($f = 103$). No other values received more than 100 endorsements. The two endorsed as the least important values were World of Beauty ($f = 76$) and National Security ($f = 70$).

The values exposed by these girls reflect what they want for themselves. The family is very important to these girls as is evident by the endorsement by 213 girls. They want to have homes that feel safe and loving. Many do not have this type of home and talked about wanting to create this type of loving environment when they grow up and have a family of their own. Also extremely important is the value of self-respect. These girls were selected by their school because they were considered at-risk for not achieving their career dreams. Valuing self-respect is a strength for these girls and can serve as a buffer against behaviors that can have negative consequences on their self respect. Like most teenagers, these girls valued their freedom and true friendship. This is highly appropriate when one considered Erikson's (1959, 1968) developmental tasks for individuals in this age group—they are supposed to be individuating and forming a separate identity. They are also at a time when friends are very important and become sources of support and influence. Finally, many of the girls reported that they were involved in sports; therefore, it is not surprising that they valued health.

Personality Profile. As discussed in the chapter on the Personality Research Form (Jackson, 1986), for 490 girls, an at-risk personality profile was evident. Mean scores were elevated for Play, Impulsivity, Defendence, Aggression, Affiliation, and Exhibition. Mean scores were depressed for Harmavoidance and Achievement. These girls could accurately be described as at-risk due to this combination of personality characteristics.

Vocational Interests. According to scores on the VPI (Holland, 1988), the highest mean work environment codes for the girls were *Investigative* ($M = 54.02$, $SD = 10.93$) and *Realistic* ($M = 53.79$, $SD = 11.24$). People who are Investigative like to work with ideas and solve problems. They are mathematician and scientists. Those who are *Realistic* like to work with their hands, outdoors, and like physics and mechanics. Engineers usually score high on *Realistic*. These two domains are representative of people who are in math, science, technology, and engineering and are happy and successful in their work. The lowest mean score was for *Social* ($M = 48.39$, $SD = $

9.50), liking to work with people and be around people. This project targeted girls who were interested in math, science, technology, or engineering. According to these results, these girls were appropriately selected and would be happy in careers that are high **Investigative** or **Realistic** and low **Social**.

Does TARGETS Impact Career Behaviors?

The second research question asked: **What are the career aspirations, behaviors, and perceived obstacles of talented at-risk girls and how are these impacted by involvement in the TARGETS program.** First, the pretest career aspirations, career search behaviors, and perceived obstacles were examined. Career aspirations were coded by amount of education needed to achieve that career goal. For the 502 girls, 123 (32%) wanted a career that would require a doctoral degree (e.g., M.D., Ph.D., J.D.), 205 (53.4%) wanted a career that required a four-year college education, and 14 (3.6%) would need at least a master's degree. Only a small number of girls had career goals that only required a high school diploma ($n = 11$, 2.2%) or some technical training ($n = 31$, 6.2%). Most of the careers identified were nontraditional ($n = 356$, 77.1%) for women.

Career behavior reflected the number of different people the girls had talked to about careers, having visited a library to look up information about careers, and having sent for information about careers. Out of a possible 11 points, the average number of people talked to was 4.24, ($SD = 2.36$). The two behaviors most endorsed were talking to parents and to friends about careers.

The most frequently mentioned **obstacle** to attaining their career dream was money ($\underline{n} = 164$, 38%). The only other obstacles mentioned by more than 30 girls included grades ($\underline{n} = 38$, 8.8%), not completing high school ($\underline{n} = 33$, 7.6%), and family ($\underline{n} = 27$, 6.3%).

While these girls had high **career aspirations**, they were currently engaged in few career search behaviors that would given them more information about careers about which they indicated they were interested. In addition, they noted several important obstacles to reaching these career goals. Many girls came from lower income families where there is little extra money for college tuition. In addition, the schools may have picked some girls who were at-risk because of grades. Certainly doing poorly in school is a realistic obstacle to career attainment and for dropping out of school. Family was also seen as an obstacle for a small percentage of the girls. Family included lack of support, family responsibilities such as needing to earn money for the family or taking care of younger siblings, and not wanting to go to school away from the family (especially true for Native American girls on the reservation).

The second half of this question asked **whether being involved in TARGETS impacted career behaviors.** Career search behavior was measured at pretest and the first follow-up. Analyses of the self-reported career search behaviors indicated that the girls reported more career search behaviors ($M = 4.82$, $SD = 2.29$) at the three to four month follow-up than they did at the pretest ($M = 4.33$, $SD = 2.32$). In addition, more girls than expected were traditional or nontraditional at both assessment times, and fewer girls than expected switched from traditional to nontraditional or switched from nontraditional to traditional. Thirteen girls switched from a traditional career aspiration to a nontraditional aspiration, and 38 switched from nontraditional to traditional. The four major obstacles remained constant at the first follow-up—money (30.6%), not graduating (14.5%), poor grades (13.3%), and family (5.2%). Money was still the most frequently mentioned obstacle at the long-term follow-up ($\underline{n}$ = 38, 56.7%).

As a result of the TARGETS program, the girls increased their seeking information about careers. The obstacles to their career goals did not change over the short follow-up but did centralize on money after several years.

Does TARGETS Impact Self-Beliefs?

Self-beliefs were defined as **self-esteem** and as **educational self-efficacy**. Both of these constructs were measured at all four time periods; however, not all girls participated at each time period. At the long-term follow-up, participants responded only to the job self-efficacy component of the self-efficacy scale.

At pretest, the mean self-esteem score for the girls was 30.06 (SD = 4.67). This is an **average self-esteem score**. Scores for the self-efficacy scales were based on a one to seven scale: Job Efficacy (M = 4.36, SD = 1.43); School Efficacy (M = 5.35, SD = 1.26); Grade Efficacy (M = 5.67, SD = 1.17); and Future Efficacy (M = 5.86, SD = .67). When math/science efficacy for school and for grades were examined, the means were 5.24 (SD = 1.35) and 5.63 (SD = 1.30), respectively. These girls are more confident about their ability to do well in school and get A's or B's and were more confident about their futures than they were about their ability to completed the needed education for various jobs. They were also relatively confident about successfully completing the coursework for and getting A or B grades in math and science classes.

The analysis conducted to determine whether **self-esteem** changed over the first three time periods (pretest, post-test, and 3-4 month follow-up). Self-esteem increased from pretest ($M = 29.25$, $SD = 4.67$) to post-test ($M = 31.52$, $SD = 5.68$) and remained stable follow-up ($M = 30.80$, $SD = 4.44$). TARGETS had a positive immediate impact of the girls' self-esteem and this impact was maintained over time.

Next, the **self-efficacy** scales were examined across pretest, post-test, and follow-up. For the 64 girls who completed the assessment of **job self-efficacy** at all three time periods, scores went up from pretest to post-test but not enough to make a difference. Job self-efficacy was only minimally impacted by the TARGETS program. Next, **school efficacy** was a lowest at the pretest ($M = 5.20$, $SD = 1.24$) and then went up at post-test ($M = 5.68$, $SD = 1.19$). This gain in school efficacy was maintained at the 3-4 month follow-up ($M = 5.47$, $SD = 1.28$).

A similar change was seen in **grade efficacy,** which increased from pretest ($M = 5.75$, $SD = .97$) to post-test ($M = 6.18$, $SD = .78$). It declined slightly at the follow-up ($M = 5.90$, $SD = 1.02$). It should be noted that the follow-up was always done at the end of a semester. This is when students are facing the reality of grades and the consequences of perhaps not working as hard as they should. Therefore, the decline in grade self-efficacy may be a result of end of semester awareness and also apprehension about end of semester exams.

Finally **future efficacy** was examined across the three time periods. Pretest future efficacy ($M = 6.21$, $SD = .60$) was lower than at post-test ($M = 6.40$, $SD = .50$). This gain in future self-efficacy was maintained at follow-up ($M = 6.30$, $SD = .63$).

These data suggest that the TARGETS had an initial positive impact on four of five self-beliefs of these girls. For **self-esteem, grade self-efficacy**, and **future self-efficacy**, there were significant increased from pre to post assessments that were maintained at the three to four month follow-up. For **school self-efficacy**, the initial gain was lost at follow-up. **Job self-efficacy** did not change across time. One objective of the TARGETS program is to reinforce and confirm the girls' academic abilities and their belief that they can do well in school. The findings indicate that this encouragement has a positive impact on the self-beliefs of the girls who completed all three assessment periods.

Does TARGETS Impact At-Risk Behaviors?

Five clusters of at-risk behaviors were assessed at the pretest. At follow-up, questions about gang activity and body image were added. Higher scores on each behavior indicates greater risk, except for exercise.

Exercise. At pretest, girls participated in average amount of **exercise** during each week. Approximate 66% of 487 girls indicated that they exercised or participated in sports three or more days each week and 66% also did stretching exercises. Slightly more than half (55.3%) walked or rode a bike three or more days per week.

Cigarettes. Although 62% of 484 girls indicated that they did not smoke **cigarettes** regularly, 71% had tried smoking. Of the 183 who considered themselves smokers, they began smoking between the ages of 13 and 14. They smoked 3 to 5 days per month and then smoked between 1 and 2 cigarettes per day.

Alcohol. At pretest, 212 (40%) indicated that they drank **alcohol** during the last month, and 196 (56%) drank alcohol during the last year. Of those who reported drinking in the last month, they drank on the average of once a week or less, for an average of once every two to three months. Most (73.1%) reported having friends who drank. Over a fourth ($n = 124$, 27.5%) self reported marijuana use and life-time other drug use. The median use of marijuana was once a week or less, while drug use did not cluster into any one time of use category but varied from 1 or 2 times per year ($n = 43$) to more than 40 times per year ($n = 31$).

Sex. Average age for initiation of **sexual behavior** was between the ages of 13 and 14 (57.6%). For those girls who had had sexual intercourse ($n = 207$, 42.6%), alcohol or drug use was involved use for 48 (23.5%) of the girls. Approximately one-fourth used no method of birth control the last time they had intercourse; although 124 (60.%) of the girls reported using the birth control pill. Approximately 13% ($n = 26$) used withdrawal as a method of birth control Of those who responded to the question about whether they had been coerced/forced to have sex the first time, 31.5% ($\underline{n} = 23$) said yes. While 88.7% had been taught about AIDS/HIV infection at school, only 62.5% had discussions about AIDS/HIV infection with their parents.

Suicide. Most of the 482 girls had **not** thought about committing **suicide** ($n = 343$, 78.6%) nor had they made a plan on how to commit suicide ($n = 382$, 78.6%). However, 61 (12.5%) had attempted suicide, with most attempting one time. Seventeen girls had attempted two or three time, six girls four or five times, and two girls reported six or more attempts. Of those who attempted suicide in the last year, 16 (3.3%) required medical care.

Gangs. Information on **gang involvement** was gathered from 159 girls. Of these 48 (30.2%) had been invited to join a gang and 17 (10.6%) joined. Most were recruited by a friend ($n = 16$) or by a family member ($n = 10$). The two primary reasons for joining a gang included protection ($n = 9$) and friendship/belonging ($n = 9$). Ten girls had been expected to commit illegal acts as a gang member.

Body Image. The final at-risk behavior assessed was **body image**. At the pretest, 249 girls were asked how they thought of themselves with respect to weight. Eight (1.6%) indicated they felt very underweight, 44 (9.1%) slightly underweight, 171 (35.3%) about right, 201 (41.4%) slightly overweight, and 61 (12.2%) very overweight. Additional body image measures were included to assess body perceptions, appearance dissatisfaction, and weight dissatisfaction. Among 238 girls, their real body was perceived as an about of two sizes ($M = 1.73$, $SD = 1.89$) larger than their ideal body. On a scale of 0 to 100, the mean appearance dissatisfaction was 44.67 ($SD = 27.91$) and the mean weight dissatisfaction was 39.90 ($SD = 25.19$).

These descriptive statistics indicate that the girls who attended TARGETS were at-risk for a variety of behaviors that could negatively impact their lives. Although most practiced healthy exercise behaviors, they tended to have a negative body image. Many drank alcohol or used marijuana and other drugs, were cigarette smokers, and had already initiated sexual behavior. Several had attempted suicide and belonged to a gang.

One of TARGETS's goals was to have a positive impact on the at-risk behaviors of these girls. It had no impact on **exercise**. When **cigarette use** was examined, use remained stable from the post-test to the follow-up. At the 3–5 year follow-up, more girls were smokers than at post-test. This may have been due to age. Most of the girls at the long-term follow-up were now young adults and smoking was no longer illegal behavior for them.

Substance use. Substance use encompassed both alcohol and other drugs. The girls' substance use remained stable from pretest to post-test to the 3-4 month follow-up. However a at the 3 –5 year follow-up, the highest substance use was found. Again, this may very well be to age and drinking becoming legal.

Sex. The same pattern that was found for cigarettes and substance use was found for sexual behaviors. When the girls were teenagers, sexual behavior remained constant. As they grew older, their sexual behaviors increased as would be expected.

Suicidality. For the 175 girls who responded to the suicide questions at pretest and first follow-up, there was a **significant decrease in suicidality**. Suicidality further decreased at the long-term follow-up.

Body Image. When **body image** was examined across time, differences were found among the three time periods (pretest, first follow-up, and long-term follow-up).

Gang. Gang involvement remained stable between the pretest and first follow-up. No long-term follow-up of gang involvement was conducted.

These data indicated that the TARGETS program had *minimal impact on at-risk behaviors except for suicidality*. This finding alone is highly important. Fewer girls were thinking about, planning, and acting on their plans to commit suicide. The trend was a continued decrease in suicidality across the three time periods. Most of the at-risk behaviors were not impacted over a short time period and actually increased two to five years post TARGETS. A realistic interpretation of this finding is that the girls were growing up and as young adults, they were much more likely to drink and try drugs, to smoke cigarettes, and to become sexually active.

Summary of Evaluation of TARGETS

The TARGETS project touched the lives of over 500 girls. The real impact was on the career aspirations and self-beliefs of these talented at-risk girls. After TARGETS involvement, they reported more career search behaviors that would increase their knowledge about careers in mathematics and science. Their self-esteem, school self-efficacy, and future self-efficacy increased from pretest to the 3 to 4 month follow-up. Because the literature is clear that increasing self concept and increasing career identity are associated with persistence in math and science, there is reason to believe that this intervention may preserve young womens' interest in these fields. In addition, their suicidality decreased over time. These findings generally support the ability of TARGETS to influence positively their career-related behaviors and attitudes regarding their own abilities to accomplish education-related tasks in math and science. Since attitudes are precursors to behaviors, this demonstrates a significant impact on the lives of these girls.

References:

Holland, J. L. (1988). *The Vocational Preference Inventory.* Odessa, FL: Psychological Assessment Resources.

Jackson, D. N. (1989). *The Personality Research Form.* Port Huron, MI: Research Psychologists Press.

Kerr, B. A. (1981). *Career education for the gifted and talented.* Columbus, OH: National Center for Research in Vocational Education. (ERIC Document Reproductions Services No. ED 205-778).

Kerr, B. A., & Erb, C. A. (1991). Career counseling with academically talented students: Effects of a value-based intervention. *Journal of Counseling Psychology, 38* (3), 309-314.

Robinson, S. E. (1992a). *Adolescent At-Risk Behaviors Inventory.* Unpublished test. Tempe, AZ: Arizona State University.

Robinson, S. E. (1992b). *Educational Self-Efficacy Scale—Adolescents.* Unpublished test. Tempe, AZ: Arizona State University.

Rokeach, M. (1967). *Value Survey.* Palo Alto, CA: Consulting Psychologists Press.

Rosenberg, M. (1965). *Society and the adolescent self-image.* Princeton, NJ: Princeton University Press.

8

Outcomes of the GEOS Program

Sarah E. Lowery
Sharon E. Robinson Kurpius
Barbara Kerr

Each year during a three-year National Science Foundation (NSF) (Kerr & Robinson Kurpius, 2000) funded project, women from the Barrett Honors College at ASU were recruited to participate in career intervention workshops entitled Gender Equity Options in Science (GEOS). GEOS participants ranged in age from 17 to 21 years with a mean age of 18.2 years (SD = .68). The majority were Euro-American ($n = 137$, 81.5%), although there also were 12 (7.1%) Latinas, 8 (4.8%) Asian Americans, 2 (1.2%) Native Americans, and one (.65) African-American involved in this project. Of those who specified where they lived, 136 reported that they lived on campus and 31 lived off-campus. Approximately one-third of their mothers and one-third of their fathers held a bachelor's degree. The jobs held by fathers and mothers were coded for traditionality. For mothers, 125 (76.2%) held traditionally female jobs (those for which the majority of the workers are women, e.g., nursing, teachers, flight attendant, or secretary). For fathers, 152 (93.3%) held jobs traditionally held by men (those for which the majority

159

of the workers are men, e.g., construction worker, police officer, doctor, or engineer). When yearly family income was examined, the median income was $80,000-$99,999 per year.

At pretest, 83 (49.7%) of the 168 women had declared a major in science, technology, engineering, or math (STEM), 66 (39.5%) had declared a non-STEM major (e.g., English, Art History), and 18 (10.8%) women were undecided. In contrast, when asked about career goals, 107 (63.7%) indicated a STEM career goal, 60 (35.7%) indicated a non-STEM career goal, and one person (.6%) was undecided.

The GEOS project used a quasi-experimental design with treatment and waitlist control groups with assessments over three time periods—pre-test, four-month follow-up, and 8 month follow-up. Approximately 50 freshman women participated in GEOS in the first year, 70 the second year, and 48 third year. Over the three years, 89 women were included in the GEOS intervention, 61 in the waitlist control group, and 18 did not complete the program and were classified as "other." Those in the waitlist control group received the GEOS intervention during the second semester of each year.

GEOS Intervention

At the beginning of each fall semester, all freshman Honors college women (approximately 200 each year) were sent letters inviting them to a formal recruiting banquet. During the banquet, prominent women speakers presented brief lectures about topics relevant to women in the sciences. In addition, the GEOS workshops were introduced, and young women interested in pursuing majors in math or the sciences or related to science (e.g., scientific artist, writer) were recruited to participate. They were told that GEOS would provide them with two three-hour workshops that would include career counseling and mentoring and would help to create community with other freshmen women interested in the sciences. At the close of the banquet, women were given pretests, and all women who wanted to join GEOS rank-ordered their preferences for workshop times from a list of days and times. During the following week, the young women were randomly assigned to treatment (fall workshops) and waitlist control (spring workshops). The treatment group was then assigned to workshop times based on their class schedules.

During Workshop I, the young women were provided with lunch or dinner. They were introduced to staff, took two assessments, and participated in a guided visualization about a perfect workday 10 years in the future. Workshop II occurred one week after the first workshop. During the second workshop, they again had lunch or dinner, completed two more assessments, and were then divided into two groups. Half received their career counseling session while the other half participated in a group that focused on a discussion of health/wellness behaviors. After an hour, the groups switched so that each woman received both components. After both workshops, GEOS women were told they would be contacted by GEOS staff in approximately four months for follow-up.

In December, all GEOS women were invited to a holiday party held at the campus student union. During this party, they completed a posttest that included questions regarding current career goals and majors, social support, commitment to completing school, and commitment to their career goals. Alternative arrangements were made (e.g., meeting in the dorms) for those GEOS women who could not come to the holiday party to fill out the posttest. In the spring semester, all waitlist control women were invited to participate in the workshops that followed a parallel pattern to those offered in the fall.

In late April of each year, all GEOS women were invited to a nearby desert ranch to take part in a 24-hour overnight retreat where they were again post-tested. Those unable to attend were contacted individually to complete the second posttest.

Outcome Variables

In addition to demographics, questions were asked about their future school plans (e.g., majors) and career goals, career search behaviors, social support (e.g., mentoring), and commitment to obtaining their education. Other assessments included the Rosenberg Self-Esteem Scale (Rosenberg, 1965, 2001), the University Environment Scale (UES; Gloria & Robinson Kurpius, 1996) Cultural Congruity Scale (CCS; Gloria & Robinson Kurpius, 1996), the College Self-Efficacy Inventory (Solberg, O'Brien, Villareal, Kennel, & Davis, 1993), the Educational Degree Behaviors Self-Efficacy Scale (EDBSES; Gloria & Robinson Kurpius, 1999), and the Persistence Voluntary Dropout Decision Scale (P/VDD Pascarella & Terenzini, 1980).

STEM majors and careers. To assess the rate of STEM major choices and STEM career aspirations, participants were asked questions regarding their current and future plans. Questions included, "What careers have you thought about pursuing?" and "What is your career goal?" The women were also asked to identify their projected or declared college major/s. In order to obtain outcome data regarding the impact of the intervention, the majors were categorized as STEM/Non-STEM based on the type of major (e.g., Physics = STEM, English =

Non-STEM). Careers were also classified as STEM/Non-STEM. Two raters performed the classifications and disagreements were discussed until consensus was obtained.

Mentoring. The women's perceptions of mentoring were assessed using the Mentoring Scale (Gloria & Robinson Kurpius, 1999). This five-item scale asks if there has been someone on campus who a) has been encouraging, b) has taken them "under their wing," c) has been a mentor, d) has cared about their educational success, and e) has been someone with whom they could identify as a role model. The Cronbach alpha was .66.

Career Search Behaviors. Career search behaviors were assessed using a revised version of the Career Exploration Activity Inventory developed for TARGETS (Kerr & Robinson Kurpius, 1994). Fifteen yes/no questions were used to measure career search behaviors. For example, students indicated whether they had visited the library and read about careers and with whom they had talked, such as counselors, teachers, and parents about career plans. The career search behavior scores could range from zero to 15. The internal consistency for the career search behaviors scale was .66 for the GEOS women.

Personal Valuing of Education. The women's valuing of education was measured using the 4-item Personal Valuing of Education Scale (Gloria, 1993). Three questions ask to what extent getting a college degree is worth the work/effort, time, and money required to obtain it. The fourth question asks how strong their commitment was to earning a bachelor's degree. Scores were obtained by summing responses and taking the average. For the GEOS women, the Cronbach alpha was .64 for the four items.

Self-Esteem. The Rosenberg Self-Esteem Scale is a 10-item scale utilized to measure overall feelings of self-worth or self-acceptance (Rosenberg, 1965). A sample item was "I am able to do things as well as most other people." For the GEOS women, the Cronbach alpha for the ten items was .84 at pretest.

Education Self-Efficacy Inventory. Two instruments were utilized to measure education self-efficacy. Two subscales (Course Self-Efficay and Social Efficacy) of the College Self-Efficacy Inventory (CSEI; Solberg et al., 1993) measured statements such as "Ask a professor a question" (Social Efficacy) and "Take good class notes" (Course Efficacy). Each item was rated on a 7-point Likert type scale. Scores across the 14 items were summed and then averaged so that higher scores indicated greater educational self-efficacy. The Cronbach alpha for the Course and Social Efficacy items combined for this study was .91 at pretest.

The second measure used to assess educational self-efficacy was the Educational Degree Behaviors Self-Efficacy Scale (EDBSES). The scale consists of 14 items that examine students' self-confidence in their ability to complete academic tasks such as "Complete the science general studies requirements with a B or better" and "Be accepted into your academic major." Items were responded to on a 7-point Likert-type scale ranging from 1 (no confidence at all) to 7 (complete confidence). Total scores were again obtained by summing and then averaging the responses. Higher scores indicated higher educational self-efficacy. For the GEOS women, the Cronbach alpha was .62.

The correlation between the two measures of self-efficacy was .58 (p = .001). Based on this strong correlation and precedence in the literature (Gloria & Robinson Kurpius, 1999), the two scales were combined by adding across the 28 items and then calculating an average score. The Cronbach alpha for the combined scales was .84.

University Environment. Again, two measures were used to assess the participants' perception of the university environment. The *Cultural Congruity Scale* (CCS; Gloria & Robinson Kurpius, 1996) was developed after a review of both the conceptual and empirical literature related to students' sense of cultural fit within the college environment. Sample items include "I can talk to my friends at school about my family and my culture" and "My ethnic values are in conflict with what is expected at school." For this study, an additional two items were deleted because they referred only to ethnic minorities and were not pertinent to the majority of GEOS women, One item was "As an ethnic minority I feel as if I belong on this campus." The second item was "I feel accepted at school as an ethnic minority." Scores across the 11 items were summed and averaged so that a total score could range from one to seven with higher scores indicating greater perceived cultural congruity. For the young women in the GEOS program, the Cronbach alpha for the 11-item scale was .75.

The second scale utilized to assess participants' perceptions of the university environment was the *University Environment Scale* (UES; Gloria & Robinson Kurpius, 1996). Sample items include "Class sizes are so large that I feel like a number" and "I feel as if no one cares about me personally on this campus." The items utilize a 7-point Likert-type response format ranging from (1) *Not at all* to (7) *Very true.* The Cronbach alpha for perceptions of the university items for the GEOS women was .84.

Academic Persistence. The Persistence/Voluntary Dropout Decisions Scale (P/VDD) was developed by Pascarella and Terenzini (1980) to assess the persistence decisions of college students. Sample items include, "It is likely I will register at the university next fall" and "It is not important to me to graduate from this university." Participants responded to the 30 items using a 5-point Likert-type response format ranging from 1 (strongly disagree) to 5 (strongly agree). Responses were summed and averaged with higher scores indicating more positive persistence decisions. The Cronbach alpha for the GEOS women was 87.

Other Instruments and Activities Used in GEOS Workshops.

Psychological instruments were used during the GEOS workshops and year-end retreats to help foster discussion and create a meaningful intervention for students. Participants completed the *Rokeach Value Survey* (Rokeach, 1967, 1973), the *Vocational Preference Inventory* (Holland, 1985a, 1985b), and the *Personality Research Form* (Jackson 1987). Participants also completed the *Weight and Appearance Visual Analogue Scales* (Heinberg & Thompson, 1995), the *Contour Drawing Rating Scale* (Thompson & Gray, 1995), and measures of health behaviors and physical fitness/health. They also participated in the Future Day Fantasy (Zunker, 1983).

During the counseling sessions participants completed a goal sheet that included questions: a) The goal, b) When do I want to reach this goal? c) What can I do by next week? d) What can I do by next month? e) What can I do within the semester? f) What obstacles may get in my way? g) What will I do to reward myself when I have reached my goal? Goal sheets were used to facilitate discussion and create a contract with GEOS women to work toward something positively related to their physical, mental, or academic health. At the desert retreat, the women participated in the Role-Stripping (Zunker, 1983) exercise. The women were asked to list their four most valued roles in order of importance (e.g., student, daughter, friend). Next, they were asked to "discard" each of the roles, one by one, going around the group and discussing in turn each role and the feelings surrounding giving up that role. When all the roles has been "stripped," the group leaders explained the value of relating important roles to career choices.

Settings for GEOS

The GEOS workshops were held in the Counselor Training Center affiliated with the Counseling and Counseling Psychology programs at Arizona State University. Past experience with talented STEM women made the researchers aware of the importance of utilizing the out-of-doors and social activities to promote women-friendly science. In addition to the two-day GEOS workshops conducted on campus, GEOS retreats were held at the end of each year at a nearby desert ranch. These natural-setting retreats provided opportunities for hands-on activities and offered a non-threatening setting that promoted student-faculty interaction.

Counselors

Over the three years of the project, 30 female graduate-level counselors-in-training who had had at least one semester of master's level practicum experience were recruited to counsel GEOS women. Each year, the counselors received a 4-hour training session conducted by the graduate assistants working for the GEOS project. The training consisted of a lecture on the obstacles college women in STEM majors may face. They also received training on how to score and interpret the workshop-related instruments. In addition, GEOS counselors participated in a role-play of a career counseling session similar to the one they would provide to the GEOS women during the GEOS workshops. Counselors were allowed to count the hours devoted to GEOS as hours toward their required clinical experiences.

The Impact of the GEOS Program

It was predicted that women who participated in the GEOS intervention would exhibit significantly higher self-beliefs than women who were in the waitlist control group. Self-beliefs were defined as self-esteem and as educational self-efficacy. All women, regardless of GEOS group, reported higher self-esteem at post-test ($M = 34.23$, $SD = 4.31$) than at pretest ($M = 33.39$, $SD = 4.64$). When educational self-efficacy was examined, all women improved their educational self-efficacy from pretest ($M = 5.99$, $SD = .66$) to post-test ($M = 6.20$, $SD = .59$). However, the GEOS intervention women reported significantly improved educational self-efficacy at the post-test as compared to the waitlist control women. These findings suggest that the GEOS intervention significantly impacted educational self-efficacy.

It was also predicted that women who participated in the GEOS intervention would have more positive perceptions of the university than would women in the waitlist control group. The GEOS intervention did not impact perceptions of the university; however, all women had more positive perceptions of the university over time.

It was also expected that women who participated in the GEOS intervention would have more positive perceptions of being mentored than would women in the waitlist control group. Mentoring was defined as perceptions of being encouraged and supported by one or more individuals on campus and total scores could range from zero to two. When GEOS women were compared at pretest and post-test, they believed that they were receiving more mentoring at post-test. Although the waitlist control women also perceived more mentoring at post-test than at pretest, the strength of this differences was not as strong as that for the GEOS women.

Personal valuing of education, academic persistence decisions, and career search behaviors were also examined. Those in the GEOS group tended to make more positive persistence decisions at the post-test as compared to the waitlist women. Both groups highly valued their education. Both groups conducted similar career search activities.

When STEM and non-STEM careers were examined, the proportion (.38) of GEOS women who chose STEM careers at both pre and post-test was significantly greater than the hypothesized proportion (.24) of women. For GEOS women who chose non-STEM careers, the proportion who maintained this choice at post-test was .38, whereas the expected proportion was .20. When majors—STEM, non-STEM, or Undecided— were examined across pretest and post-test, the proportion (.33) of GEOS women who chose STEM majors at both pre and post-test was significantly greater than the hypothesized proportion (.13) of women. For GEOS women who chose non-STEM majors, the proportion who maintained this choice at post-test was .50, whereas the expected proportion was .20. Both the number of women who chose STEM career goals and majors was larger than the hypothesized number. It should be noted that for the women in the GEOS intervention, self-beliefs, mentoring, perceptions of the university environment, and choice of STEM majors and careers were maintained from the post-assessment to the follow-up assessment.

Since the waitlist control group received the GEOS intervention after they were post-tested, their career choices and majors at pretest and at follow up were examined to determine whether they were impacted by the GEOS intervention. Of the 167 women who reported a major at pretest, 18% ($n = 30$) of waitlist women and 26.9% ($n = 45$) of GEOS women reported STEM majors. Of the 76 women who completed the follow up, 28.9% ($n = 22$) of the waitlist women and 31.6% ($n = 24$) of the original GEOS group reported STEM majors. At pretest, 44.9% of all women chose STEM majors. At follow up, 60.5% of the still participating women chose STEM majors.

A similar analysis was conducted on career goals. For the 168 women who reported career goals at pretest, 22% ($n = 37$) of the waitlist women and 34.5% ($n = 58$) of the GEOS group reported STEM career goals. At follow up, 77 women reported career goals. Of these, 33.8% ($n = 26$) of the waitlist group and 31.2% ($n = 24$) of the original GEOS group chose STEM career goals. Overall, at follow up, after everyone had received the GEOS intervention, 65% of those still participating chose STEM career goals.

Finally, the ability of pretest scores on self-esteem, educational self-efficacy, perceptions of the university environment, cultural congruity, and perceptions of being mentored to predict academic persistence decisions was tested. Three variables—perceptions of the university environment, mentoring, and educational self-efficacy accounted for 54.5% of the variance in academic persistence decisions. Academic persistence decisions were positively related to perceptions of the university environment ($r = .68$, $p = .001$), to educational self-efficacy ($r = .40$, $p = .001$), and to perceptions of being mentored ($r = .46$, $p = .001$). Participants who viewed the university environment as more warm and accepting, who had higher educational self-efficacy, and who believed that at least one person on campus cared and supported them, the more positive their decisions about persisting in school. Even though academic persistence decisions were positively related to cultural congruity ($r = .28$, $p = .001$) and to self-esteem ($r = .31$, $p = .001$), they did not enhance the predictive ability of the regression equation.

Profile of a typical GEOS girl

The GEOS data revealed interesting information regarding the profile of a "typical" GEOS woman. To create this profile, responses to the pretest assessments including demographic characteristics and educational and career aspirations were averaged. A typical GEOS woman is an 18 year old Euro-American freshman with a projected STEM major. She is from a two-parent home with a yearly income of $89,999-$99,999. She is likely to have two siblings. Both her mother and father have bachelor's degrees and likely are in professions that are traditional to their genders (e.g., dad is a doctor, mom is a nurse). Her most important values include family security, true friendship, and spirituality. She plans to get married, have children, and have a career. A typical GEOS woman has a Holland interest code of Artistic, Investigative, and Social (AIS), indicating that the women scored highest for Artistic, second highest for Investigative, and third highest for Social. Her giftedness and creativity are reflected through the elevated "A" scale which reflects careers such as poet and painter. Her interest in science as well as her inquisitive traits is reflected through her elevated "I" score. Investigative careers include careers such as professor and scientist. Her caring nature, enjoyment of people, and feminine socialization predispose her for an interest in social careers, "S." Social careers might include being a teacher, psychologist, and social worker. She reports that her ideal career is working in the medical field as a doctor or researcher. She sees actually getting through school and getting good grades as major career obstacles. Overall, the profile of a typical GEOS woman reflects an intelligent young woman who has a passion for a non-traditional STEM career but is quite aware of possible obstacles she may face in obtaining her career goals.

Summary and Implications for Counselors

In addition to the maintenance of educational self-efficacy and perceptions of mentoring, more women who had received the GEOS program intervention than expected persisted in their choices of STEM careers and majors. This finding has special importance given that approximately 50% of students entering college with an intention to major in STEM, change majors within the first two years, with women receiving far fewer STEM degrees than men (National Science Board, 2002; National Science Foundation, 2000). Furthermore, the finding supports previous research suggesting that interventions that occur early in students' education and that target the specific needs of women have been shown to increase persistence rates in STEM majors (Nauta, Epperson, & Kahn, 1998; Schaefers, Epperson, & Nauta., 1997)

The GEOS intervention positively impacted decisions related to choice of STEM careers and majors. Terenzini and Wright (1987) argued that the academic major provides an important sense of identity for students and is the primary academically-based peer grouping supported by the institution. The GEOS intervention served to broaden academic peer groupings and reinforce students' commitment to STEM majors. That is, the banquets, workshops, retreats, and follow-up parties may have provided the women with a sense of community in relation to their STEM majors. In terms of career commitment, researchers have noted a clear connection between perceived barriers and career outcomes (Brown & Lent, 1996, 1999). Additionally, Brown and Krane (2000) argued that interventions that focus on reducing barriers to certain career attainment may not be as effective as efforts aimed at increasing support networks of those in the process of pursing careers choices.

The GEOS program was a positive intervention in that it provided resources that allowed the women to be in contact with peers, mentors, and professors interested in STEM majors and careers (Kerr & Robinson Kurpius, 2004). While some of the possible barriers to achievement in STEM majors and careers were addressed, the majority of the intervention focused on providing women with encouragement and with the necessary support systems and tools needed to persist in pursuing STEM careers.

The GEOS intervention had a positive impact on educational self-efficacy and perceptions of mentoring, and more women who received the GEOS program than expected persisted in their choices of STEM careers and majors. Additionally, for all women in the study, perceptions of the university environment, educational self-efficacy and perceptions of being mentored were each positively related to academic persistence decisions. Overall, this study was unique in that it provided talented, freshman women enrolled in an Honors program with a psychosocial intervention that targeted their perceptions and decisions. This study supports the literature on academic persistence that has found that a positive university environment (e.g., comfort, support) and belief in one's academic abilities positively impact academic persistence decisions. The GEOS study is distinct in that the specific GEOS career intervention positively impacted educational self-efficacy and perceptions of mentoring for the treatment group, as well as choices of STEM careers and majors. Through the GEOS program, the women gained access to social support, encouragement, information on STEM careers, positive STEM role models, peer support, and specialized career and personality assessments.

Women are still underrepresented in STEM fields (NSF; 2000), particularly in the physical sciences, mathematics, technology, and engineering (National Science Board, 2002). Women continue to be subjected to stereotypes regarding their abilities to achieve in STEM fields (Robinson Kurpius, 2002; Robinson Kurpius, Krause, Yasar, Roberts, & Baker, 2004) and may even be discouraged from developing interests in fields such as computing and engineering (Margolis, 2002; Robinson Kurpius & Kerr, 2001). Most young women interested in STEM fields may not have access to interventions that will positively impact their persistence in STEM majors and careers (Chang, 2002). However, many college women may seek guidance from counseling psychologists at university career centers or counseling services, from professors and other university staff.

In terms of future directions for counseling, the GEOS study provides evidence for the influence of support and encouragement, a comfortable university environment, and educational self-efficacy on academic persistence decisions. Furthermore, the GEOS intervention had a positive impact on educational self-efficacy and perceptions of mentoring. Counselors may play an important role in providing support and encouragement for women interested in STEM majors and careers (Robinson Kurpius & Kerr, 2000). It is vital that individual career and university psychologists be aware of the many obstacles that young women may face when pursuing a career in STEM. Group counseling may also be helpful for young women interested in STEM majors and careers. Women seem to benefit from sharing their experiences with peers to help normalize their feelings (Brown & Lent, 1996; Chartrand & Rose, 1996). When sharing with peers, women may also find they are not alone in feeling frustrated by difficult course material or professors who do not encourage women to stay in STEM fields (Robinson Kurpius et al., 2004). Talking with other women interested in STEM may make these young women less likely to attribute their academic challenges to a lack of ability (Nauta et al., 1998).

In summary, this project highlights the importance of educational self-efficacy and mentoring for women's persistence in STEM majors and careers. Hopefully, individual and group interventions based on the study's findings will help increase the number of women who are able to pursue their dreams and excel in a STEM career.

References:

Brown, S. D., & Lent, R. W. (1996). A social cognitive framework for career choice counseling. *The Career Development Quarterly, 44,* 354-366.

Brown, S.D., & Lent, R. W. (1999). *The role of context in career choice: Theoretical elaborations and practical applications.* Paper presented at the Fourth Biennial Conference of the Society for Vocational Psychology, Milwaukee, WI.

Brown, S. D., & Krane, N. R. (2000). Four (or five) sessions and a cloud of dust: Old assumptions and new observations about career counseling. In S. D. Brown & R. W. Lent (Eds.), *Handbook of Counseling Psychology,* (3rd ed., pp.740-766). New York: Wiley.

Chang, J. C. (2002). *Women and minorities in the science, mathematics and engineering pipeline* (Report No. EDO-JC-02-06). Washington, DC: Office of Educational Research and Improvement. (ERIC Document Reproduction Service No. ED467855).

Chartrand, J. M., & Rose, M. L. (1996). Career interventions for at-risk populations: Incorporating social cognitive influences. *The Career Development Quarterly, 44,* 341-353.

Gloria, A. M. & Robinson Kurpius, S. E. (1996). The validation of the cultural congruity scale and the university environment scale with Chicano/a students. *Hispanic Journal of Behavioral Sciences, 18*(4), 533-549.

Gloria, A. M., & Robinson Kurpius, S. E. (2001). Influences of self-beliefs, social support, and comfort in the university environment on the academic nonpersistence decisions of American Indian undergraduates. *Cultural Diversity and Ethnic Minority Psychology, 7*(1), 88-102.

Gloria, A. M., & Robinson Kurpius, S. E. (1999). African American students' persistence at a predominately white university: Influences of social support, university comfort, and self-beliefs. *Journal of College Student Development, 40* (3), 257-268.

Heinberg, L. J., & Thompson, J. K. (1995). Body image and televised images of thinness and attractiveness. *Journal of Social and Clinical Psychology, 14*, 325-338.

Holland, J. L. (1985). *Vocational Preference Inventory (VPI)*. Odessa, FL: Psychological Assessment Resources.

Holland, J. L. (1985). *Vocational Preference Inventory (VPI: Professional manual.* Odessa, FL: Psychological Assessment Resources.

Jackson, D. N. (1987). *Personality Research Form—Form E. Manuel.* Port Huron, MI: Sigma Assessment Systems.

Kerr, B. A. & Robinson Kurpius, S. E. (2004). Encouraging talented girls in math and science; Effects of a guidance intervention. *High Abilities Studies, 15*, 85-102.

Kerr, B. A. & Robinson Kurpius, S. E. (1997*). Guiding Girls into Math and Science (GEMS).* Grant funded by the National Science Foundation.

Kerr, B. A. & Robinson Kurpius, S. E. (1994*). Talented At Risk Girls: Encouragement and Training for Sophomores (TARGETS).*Grant funded by the National Science Foundation.

Kerr, B. A. & Robinson Kurpius, S. E. (2000). *Gender Equity Options in Science.* Grant funded by the National Science Foundation.

Margolis, J. (2002). *Unlocking the clubhouse: Women in computing.* Cambridge, MA: The MIT Press.

National Science Board (2002). *Science and engineering indicators-2002*, (Report No. NSB-02-1). Arlington, VA: Author.

National Science Foundation (2000). *Women, minorities, and persons with disabilities in science and engineering: 2000* (Report No. NSF 00-327). Arlington, VA. (ERIC Document Reproduction Service Number ED 128 764).

Nauta, M. M., Epperson, D. L., & Kahn, J. H. (1998). A multiple groups analysis of predictors of higher-level career aspirations among women in mathematics, sciences and engineering majors. *Journal of Counseling Psychology, 45*(4), 483-496.

Pascarella, E. T., & Terenzini, P. T. (1980). Predicting freshman persistence and voluntary dropout decisions from a theoretical model. *Journal of Higher Education, 51,* 60-75.

Robinson Kurpius, S. E. (2002). *Psychosocial Factors in the Lives of College Freshmen, Vice Presidential Address,* Paper presented at the American Educational Research Association Annual Conference, New Orleans, LA.

Robinson Kurpius, S. E., & Kerr, B. A. (2000*). TARGETS: An intervention program for talented at-risk girls.* Paper presented at the annual meeting of the American Educational Research Association, New Orleans, LA.

Robinson Kurpius, S. E., & Kerr, B. A. (2001). *Guiding girls into engineering math and science.* Paper presented at the American Educational Research Association Annual Meeting, Seattle, WA.

Robinson Kurpius, S. E., Krause, S., Yasar, S, Roberts, C., & Baker, D. (2004). *Assessing DET in schools.* Paper presented at the National Association of Research in Science Teaching, Vancouver, Canada.

Rokeach, M. (1967). *Value Survey.* Palo Alto, CA: Consulting Psychologists Press.

Rokeach, M. (1973). *The nature of human values.* New York: Free Press.

Rosenberg, M. (1965). *Society and the adolescent self-image.* Princeton, NJ: Princeton University Press.

Rosenberg, M. (2001). Self-concept research: A historical overview. *Social Forces, 68*(1), 34-44

Schaefers, K. G., Epperson, D. L., & Nauta, M. M. (1997). Women's career development: Can theoretically derived variables predict persistence in engineering majors? *Journal of Counseling Psychology, 44*(2), 173-183.

Solberg, V. S., O'Brien, K., Villareal, P., Kenner, R., & Davis, A. (1993). Self-Efficacy and Hispanic college students: Validation of the College Self-Efficacy Instrument. *Hispanic Journal of Behavioral Sciences, 15,* 80-95.

Terenzini, P. T., & Wright, T. M. (1987). Influences on students' academic growth during four years of college. *Research in Higher Education, 26*(2), 161-179.

Thompson, J. K., & Gray, J. J. (1995). Development and validation of a new body image assessment scale. *Journal of Personality Assessment, 64,* 258-269.

Zunker, A. (1983). *Career Counseling.* Monterey, CA: Brooks/Cole.

9

A Qualitative Follow-up of the GEOS Project: A Success Story

Alison Toren

Although quantitative data can provide a great deal of information about the GEOS project, it cannot provide the whole picture. For a fuller portrait, we must turn to qualitative data. The GEOS project, begun in 2000 (Kerr & Robinson Kurpius, 2000) had as its goals the creation of a safe and friendly environment for career exploration, as well as providing an opportunity for developing mentoring relationships and expanding participants' support systems. This chapter will detail the results of a qualitative study that was conducted for the purpose of determining the degree to which these goals were fulfilled.

In order to conduct this study, files of GEOS participants were examined to identify those for whom we had a complete and current e-mail address. The research team also developed several open ended questions. A survey that included the open ended questions and the demographic information was developed using a web-based survey creation program.

An e-mail containing a link to the survey was sent to 102 young women who had gone through the GEOS program. They clicked on the link provided in the e-mail in order to complete the survey. Forty-six women who had participated in GEOS responded to our e-mail. Twenty were now seniors, 17 were juniors, 8 sophomores, and one was now a graduate student. The racial/ethnic distribution for these women included 39 Euro-American, 3 Asian American, 2 Hispanic, 1 African American, 1 Native American, and one unidentified. Of these 46, 42 completed all or nearly all of the questions. The average respondent to this survey was now a 21 year old, Euro-American woman, with a science, engineering, technology or math (STEM) major, who was a senior, and planned on graduating in the spring of 2004.

The questions were analyzed using qualitative sorting procedures. Each statement was examined in order to determine the theme or themes present. Each statement was then classified with other similar statements. Because of the open ended nature of the questions, some responses contained multiple themes and were, therefore, placed in all categories in which they fit. Because of this, the percentages presented in the study may not equal 100%.

Q1: What is/was your college major?

The GEOS project was designed to provide young women with the support and personal resources to complete STEM majors. Of the 42 individuals who identified their college major, 29 (69%) indicated they currently are completing a STEM major. Of these 29 women their STEM majors include:

- Bioengineering, 7 women
- Engineering (chemical or aerospace), 6 women
- Biology, 5 women

- Architechture, 3 women
- Social science/psychology, 5 women

Other majors that were identified in this study include non-experimental social science areas such as political science and history (n = 4, 9.5%), arts/design related fields (n = 2, 5%), business/marketing majors (n = 4, 9.5%), and majors in communication or foreign languages (n = 3, 7%).

Q2: What is/was your college minor?

In this study, 16 women indicated that they had chosen a college minor. Four (25%) women reported that they have chosen STEM minors such as psychology or pre-med. Other minors that were chosen included communication or languages (n = 5, 31%), business related (n = 3, 19%), humanities (n = 3, 19%) and design studies (n = 1, 6%). It appears that the majority of the women in this study have either not yet chosen a minor or do not plan on doing so.

Q3: What was you career dream when you participated in GEOS?

We asked the GEOS participants to recall what their career goals were when they went through the program. Thirty-seven women answered this question. After assessing the responses, the results indicated that 24 (64.9%) of the women began GEOS with a STEM career as their goal. For example, 5 women wanted to become some form of medical doctor, four women wanted a career in bioengineering, and 3 women wanted to become an architect. In addition, three women recalled having an art or design related career goal such as becoming a graphic designer or photographer. Other goals included careers focused on writing or editing such as journalism or magazine editor, and careers related to the non-experimental social sciences such as becoming a history teacher or a politician. Furthermore, 12 (32.4%) women reported having career goals that required a graduate or professional degree, such as attending medical school or becoming a clinical psychologist. While participating in GEOS, 3 (8.1%) of the women indicated that they did not have a career dream.

Q4: What is your current career goal?

When asked what their current career goal was, 22 (52.4%) young women indicated that they plan to enter STEM careers. Some of these career goals include becoming a dentist, a physical therapist, a pediatrician, an engineer in a medical device company, an aerospace engineer, a neuroscientist, a social psychologist, and an architect. Four (9.5%) women indicated that their current career goal related to a non-experimental social science profession such as becoming a high school counselor or history teacher. Currently, 6 (14.3%) women have design and art related career goals such as becoming an advertising executive, designing book and CD covers, and being a photography teacher. Additional goals include, business related professions such as becoming a marketing executive and communication careers such as working for a magazine or a job that allows them to use their foreign language skills. Seven (16.7%) participants indicated that they wanted a career that allowed them to teach, such as becoming a college professor. Twenty (47.6%) of the women surveyed have career goals that require a graduate or professional degree. Some of these careers include becoming a dentist, a professor of political theory, a marine biologist, a doctor, and attaining an advanced degree in engineering.

Q5: What are/have been the major obstacles to achieving your career goals?

The women perceived that the primary obstacle to achieving their career goals was due to difficulties with the academic aspects of college such as challenging coursework, excessive workload, and difficulties with professors (40.6%). One woman reported that "the biggest obstacle has been the level of work required for my courses. It seems like the work load just increases with each semester. I am also very active in student organizations, and it has been a challenge to try to balance those responsibilities with my responsibilities as a student." Another woman stated that her major obstacle was "the difficulty of the engineering curriculum". Yet another GEOS participant remarked that: "many obstacles have been present in my senior design class. Our instructor would assign 40 page reports, sometimes only one day prior to the due date. This contributed too many all-nighters and ultimately to frustration, due to his disorganized manner."

The theme of the next most prevalent obstacle related to choosing and preparing for a career mentioned by 31.2% of the women. Several women reported that taking the GRE or MCAT, applying, and getting into graduate or profession school was a major obstacle for them. Other participants indicated that they were experiencing some career indecision: "another obstacle lately has been trying to decide if this is the right field for me or not. I know I would do well in it, but am not sure that is what I want". Other obstacles that participants experienced related to financial difficulties, lack of support from significant people in their lives, lack of self-confidence, and procrastination.

Q6: What impact did GEOS have on you and your career development?

Several important positive themes emerged when looking at the participants' responses to the impact of GEOS on their career development. The first theme was **support and encouragement to achieve their career goals** and was highlighted by 13 (31%) of the participants. For instance, one women reported that "GEOS was probably one of my most memorable experiences at ASU. . . it was empowering to be around so many phenomenal women who have achieved so much in their lives. It was really inspiring and memorable." Another participant remarked that "GEOS offered an environment where I could talk to other women who were trying to reach their own goals. The support that was there in the meetings helped reassure me that whatever path I do choose to take will be fine." In addition, women frequently used adjectives like inspirational, motivating, encouraging and empowering to describe their GEOS experience.

The young women also reported that GEOS was instrumental in **helping them evaluate their career goals and interests, as well as helping them plan for the future.**, the second theme. One young woman reported that GEOS "gave me resources to properly plan my future career and education." Another participant replied by saying that "this program lets you know that you can do whatever you set your mind to. In addition, it helps you to chart the way to this dream/goal." Yet another participant observed that "the main thing that I took away from GEOS was that it is never too late to change your field of study or to change your career goals. Just because

186

I pick one career now doesn't mean I have to stick with it forever. It also made me a little more determined to go into a field of math or science because I just really do not want to be another of those statistics of women dropping out of the math and science departments."

The third theme indicated that GEOS provided an **opportunity to connect with role models, mentors, and peers** (23.8%). For instance, one woman remarked that "GEOS helped me to network with other women in non-traditional fields and talk about the obstacles that we have faced. It was helpful to know that there were others in the same boat as me. Also, GEOS helped me realize that my dreams are attainable even if I don't get all A's in my classes. I learned to look beyond today's challenges and plan for my future." Another participant reported that GEOS "gave me a push in the right direction. They provided me with the support and encouragement I needed during my freshman year. I made some great friends in the program and realized that there were other women out there struggling with the same issues as myself."

The last theme focused on **strengthening their self-confidence.** The women reported that GEOS increased their confidence in themselves (19%). One young woman recalled that GEOS helped her "more than most would know. Anytime I feel that I might not be able to make it. . .I think about the fact that I can and I will. This was a major theme for me in GEOS, and it has helped me through my college experience". The women surveyed also remarked that GEOS helped them gain knowledge about women's experience in STEM majors and careers. For example a young women responded by stating that "I think the most powerful aspect of the GEOS program was alerting me to some of the differences between men and women in relation to their education. One of the comments that were made during the program was that women tend to internalize the blame when they don't achieve at the highest level, while men tend to externalize that blame. I have found that I often fall victim to that. But because I can recognize what I am doing, I can see the blame and move past it instead of beating myself up over my failings."

Only three of the women surveyed felt that GEOS had little to no impact on their career development. The lack of impact appeared to be related to low participation levels or changing to a non STEM major and feeling that GEOS was, therefore, irrelevant to their redefined career goals. Overall, however, GEOS appeared to have a positive impact on the participants' career development.

Q7: What part of the GEOS project do you remember the most?

When participants were asked what part of the GEOS experience was most memorable, over half reported that the retreat to desert ranch at Saguaro Lake had the greatest impact on them. The retreats were designed to allow GEOS women to get away from the stresses of campus life and spend time in a relaxing environment surrounded by successful women scientists, professors, the program coordinators, and graduate assistants. One woman remarked that *"the retreat was fantastic. It was a lot of fun to spend time with such fantastic women. They seemed to know exactly how I felt and shared with us their experiences"*. Another participant felt that "the environment up there was incredible and serene. Being in a quiet environment with so much history made reflection very easy. It was really nice to have the alone time up there to think about myself and what I want. Hearing the stories of all of the women who were invited up there to speak with us was incredible as well. It was nice to have one on one time with some of them around the fire, or on the walk up to the petroglyphs in the dark."

One other memorable aspect of the GEOS program appeared to be the Future Day Fantasy exercise (31%). "The visualization exercise is the part of the program that I remember most. I can still remember where I saw myself in 10 years, and while that vision has changed over the past couple years, I understand the importance of having a vision." Participants also appeared to feel that the lunches/dinners, which included the opportunity to listen to speakers, were very valuable. One woman recalled a speaker discussing "a study that found that men go through college and become more confident in their skills, whereas women go through college and value their knowledge lower. That stuck with me, and while I am always trying to learn, I never try to doubt my knowledge."

The people involved in the program were also valued by several participants. For instance, one women responded by stating she valued "the abundant amount of warmth I received from the coordinators. Not only were they really personable and easy to talk to, but I felt very singled out in a good way. I wasn't just one of the participants, they were very good about remembering our names and information. I also remember how surprised I was that there were so many free gifts, dinners, and "treats" for us all the time. I have to admit, I was somewhat suspicious about so much money put forth toward some freshman that they didn't really know was going to help them sufficiently with their study. However, as such, it made me feel very special and needed, and I am very glad to follow up with GEOS." Other memorable portions of the GEOS program were the role stripping exercise and completing the interest inventories and receiving a career counseling session.

Q8: What was the most valuable part of the GEOS for you?

The aspect of the GEOS program that was by far the most valuable for participants appeared to be the connection made with other women in the form of role models, mentors, friends, and a support network (61.9%). For instance, one individual reported that "being able to talk about my dreams was the best part of GEOS for me. I was able to say what I really thought without anyone ever being critical or judgmental, and I felt like everyone cared about what my dreams were and supportive of me meeting them." Several women reported that they valued the support and encouragement they received from the program coordinators and the graduate assistants. Others recalled that they appreciated the friends they made as well as the opportunity to been surrounded by so many motivated and successful women. In addition, several young women commented about the importance of having role models for balancing a career and family. "The most valuable part, was just knowing how other women have coped with families and careers, because I plan on doing both."

Participants also recalled that GEOS helped them gain insight in to themselves and clarify their career direction. "The most valuable part was the clarity and confidence I gained from evaluating my goals, my personality, and the avenues I could take (and have taken) in life."

Finally, GEOS helped many women increase confidence in themselves. The words of one young woman exemplifies the impact of the GEOS program on its participants:

"I learned to think about myself and not others. It sounds somewhat harsh and selfish, but I was on the extreme of pleasing others before myself. Learning to think about what I want and knowing that that was valuable and incredibly important was probably the best aspect of GEOS for me. It was also incredible because I saw such a transformation in myself from the first year to my last year. My first year, I was a freshman with ulcers who was dependent on my boyfriend. Now I am an incredibly independent person who has learned that life will do what it may, and I needn't worry as much because decisions are not as permanent as I may sometimes think they are. There were a number of circumstances that led to this transformation; however, GEOS was a large part of this, and something that I still think about, and talk about, to this day. In fact, just a few days ago, while reminiscing about our years at ASU, GEOS was one of the first things that I mentioned on a list of memorable experiences."

After analyzing the responses of the young women who took part in the GEOS project, it is apart that the program fulfilled its goal of creating a safe and supportive environment in which participants could network with other women and develop mentoring relationships as well as friendships. The results of this study also indicate that most of the women who came to the GEOS training with STEM majors remained in those STEM majors at the follow-up. In addition, the themes of gaining support, encouragement, clarifying their career direction, and

191

increasing self-confidence were repeated over and over. Qualitative procedures have allowed us to gain deeper insight into the effect the GEOS experience has had on its participants.

Reference

Kerr, B.A., and Robinson Kurpius, S.E. (2000). *Gender Equity Options in Science.* Grant funded by the National Science Foundation

10

Conclusions:
Handbook for Counseling Girls and Women

Volumes 1 and 2

Barbara Kerr

Counseling Girls and Women, Volumes 1 and 2 provide the results of the research of ten years of studies of mathematically and scientifically talented girls. It is our hope that these volumes will serve to guide our efforts to increase the number of women entering Science, Technology, Engineering, and Math (STEM) careers. We hope to keep talented girls' career aspirations, whatever they may be, alive. However, our focus has been on STEM careers because these are the paths that talented girls are most likely to turn away from prematurely, compromising their hopes for careers that afford them higher salaries, status, and autonomy. In addition, the pool of candidates for leadership in STEM is small in the US compared to other advanced, industrialized countries. We have reached saturation levels in the male population for STEM careers – that is, recruitment efforts among male students, particularly White male students, are not likely to increase the number of students majoring in STEM careers. Therefore, most new American scientists will come from the pool of women and minority students who are considering STEM careers. In this section are provided the suggestions and materials needed to create counseling and guidance strategies to encourage girls and women to identify their talents, interests, personality characteristics and values; to envision their future; to embrace their goals; and to overcome internal and external barriers to success. The following are conclusions and suggestions based on each chapter of the two books.

Key Points from Volume 1
1. The girls that may be most likely to become accomplished scientists, mathematicians, technologists, and engineers may be those girls who have had to surmount both internal and external barriers – that is, talented at risk girls.
2. The development of a career identity requires not only that females explore various careers, but that they be encouraged to develop an identity as a scientist, mathematician, engineer, etc, in adolescence.
3. There are no differences across ethnic groups in talented girls' career aspirations; what makes the difference in whether these girls achieve their aspirations are reduced opportunities for minorities and gender socialization.
4. Native Americans may be the most economically disadvantaged group in the U.S. Therefore, talented Native American girls are less likely than other groups to be identified as promising in academic pursuits, and less likely to receive the guidance needed to achieve in STEM. Interventions require that these girls' career goals be discussed in the context of their concern for their community. Guidance must be sensitively adjusted to the

196

cultural heritage of each Native American girl; for example, counseling Navajo girls into pre-med careers must take into account traditional Navajos' avoidance of the deceased.

5. Biases in testing and definitions of giftedness insure that African American girls are sorely underrepresented in gifted programs. Guidance of African American talented girls must be based on partnerships among schools, families and communities. Oppression and poverty have often created negative scripts for these girls, and counselors must use positive scripting to change these girls' attitudes toward achievement and aspiration.

6. Asian American gifted girls struggle with the "Model Minority Myth," which insists that all Asian Americans are perfect, high achieving scholars, particularly in math. In addition, the objectification of Asian American women in the media confuses these girls about what goals are appropriate for them. Finally, families play a critical role in girls' decisions about their future. Guidance interventions must take all of these issues into account, and must avoid stereotypes that narrow girls' choices.

7. Immigration status, acculturation, gender socialization and language all play a role in the development of the "Latina Disadvantage." Marianismo, the requirement that Latinas emulate the Virgin Mary, preferring spiritual attainment to worldly attainment, may be interpreted by Latinas to mean that they should not pursue their academic goals. Guidance should be based on Latinas' strengths as moral and family leaders, as

bilingual citizens, and as young women with rich and complex perspectives.

8. White talented girls may feel as if they are outside the inside; they are privileged as whites, and yet socialized for secondary roles. Eating disorders, perfectionism, and self-esteem difficulties may pose barriers that must be overcome before career goals can be achieved.

9. Intelligent, high achieving girls may be more at risk for eating disorders than the general population. Eating disorders may pose a significant barrier to academic achievement and college persistence.

10. The sexuality of talented girls is characterized by complexity and diversity. When heterosexual or lesbian development is labeled as risky and negative, gifted girls are less likely to be empowered and feel a sense of sexual agency. Empowering girls to understand sexuality from their own perspective may generalize to other areas of empowerment, such as academic and career.

11. Parent relationships, particularly strong father attachments, can aid in the development of healthy sexuality. Both personality and decision making abilities affect decisions to engage in sexual behavior. Talented girls need to be taught effective decision making skills related to sexuality to preserve their academic and career choices.

12. The tension between a gifted girl's desire for belonging and desire for achievement can be one of the factors leading to substance abuse. In addition, stereotypes of geniuses and creative persons as substance abusers may lead talented girls to wrongly believe that substance use is part of creative life. Counselors need to dispel these

myths while sensitively understanding the motivations leading to substance use.

13. Talented girls who have high levels of aggressiveness and impulsivity and low levels of harm avoidance may be particularly at risk for suicide. The very characteristics of courage and creativity that allow talented girls to succeed can also be the characteristics that put them at risk when internal and external pressures lead to hopelessness. Counselors must make girls aware of this paradox, and help them to in prevention strategies that will direct them toward hopefulness about the future.

14. The special needs of the mobile, talented girls are likely to go unnoticed. Girls from families that are highly mobile need help forming a stable social support network, counseling for a strong sense of self, and help with forming their academic and career identity.

15. Coping strategies, goal-directedness, a strong ethnic identity, a support system of significant others, and school and community involvement are critical to the development of resilience in gifted girls. Because talented girls are more likely to be action oriented and responsive, the development of resilience may be an important protective factor.

16. There is no strong evidence that single parent families or maternal employment put talented girls more at risk. For talented at risk girls, a strong relationship with one parent can be a protective factor, leading to increased sense of responsibility and self-directedness. Counselors should use a strengths model, rather than a deficit model, in

counseling talented girls from single parent families.

17. Spiritual well being and spiritual giftedness may be important protective factors in the lives of talented at risk girls. Counselors should include spirituality in their discussions with girls about their sense of identity, purpose, and aspirations.

Key Points from Volume 2

1. Gifted girls are more likely than average girls to be developmentally advanced, to have high career aspirations, and to be academically achieving. They outperform boys in all academic areas throughout the school years. Nevertheless, they are at risk for not achieving their goals because they may camouflage their talents, lose self-esteem during teen years, and receive a less rigorous and responsive education than gifted boys.

2. Perfectionism, lack of self-efficacy, and negative self-beliefs may impair college women's pursuit of their goals. In addition, a null academic environment, a culture of romance, and a lack of mentors and role models may prevent girls from aspiring to STEM and other high level careers.

3. The TARGETS program is a comprehensive, research based set of strategies for identifying talents, interests, personality characteristics and values associated with success in STEM and other fields; for reducing risky behaviors and increasing resilience; and for helping girls to set clear college and career goals.

4. The GEOS program extends the work of the TARGETS program by adding mentoring and role models; strategies for overcoming negative campus and classroom environments; and encouragement toward persistence.

Appendix

Materials and Methods

Appendix 1

The Perfect Future Day Fantasy Script

Instructions to facilitator:

Tell the participants that you are going to take them on a trip ten years into their own future. Say that the fantasy works best when everybody allows themselves to imagine their perfect day in an uncensored fashion, not worrying about such things as whether they have the skills or finances to achieve these experiences. It also works best when everybody tries to imagine a working day, rather than simply a vacation day. Finally, the exercise is most effective when the facilitator silently imagines, *along with the girls*, her own perfect future day. Not only does this give the facilitator something to share of her own, but it also insures that she will speak the script slowly enough that everyone has time to fully visualize each component of the fantasy. When the facilitator rushes through the script, the perfect day flies by, and nobody has an opportunity to see the details of future possibilities. Allow at least thirty minutes for the visualization, and another thirty for processing the responses.

Lie back and get as comfortable as you can – take off your shoes, put your feet up, stretch out, and relax. Close your eyes and breathe deeply. Relax your feet, your legs, your back, your neck, your arms and hands, and even the muscles in your face. Now take ten deep breaths, and we will begin.

Appendix 1

Imagine that as you fall asleep one night, you are suddenly surrounded by a golden, glittering grid of light. You realize that you are in a time machine that is taking you into your own future.

It is the year Two Thousand and _____. Two Thousand and _____. Two Thousand and _____ (the facilitator goes on in this way until the year is reached that is ten years in the future.)

It is the year Two Thousand and _____, and you are waking to the most perfect day of your life. It is ten years in the future, and you are now about to live a wonderful day, a working day that you have most hoped for.

As you awaken, look out the window of your room. What is the season? .....
What is the climate?.... Where are you? .... Where in the world are you living?

Now turn to the side. On this perfect day, is there someone there with you? ... Or is this perfect day one in which you wake on your own? Are their sounds of others, or the sounds of solitudes? Are their animals or plants around you?

It's time to get up! Will you exercise, or will you go straight to your shower or bath?.... Imagine your preparation for the day.... Imagine the most lovely bathing experience, with all the fragrances that you love.

Now it's time to get dressed. Go to your closet or wardrobe, and pick out the most perfect clothes

imaginable. These are the clothes in which you look your best and feel most comfortable. The clothes that express most perfectly who you are...
Now that you are dressed, go to a mirror.

See yourself in the mirror as you appear as a woman ten years more mature. Imagine that you are as strong and healthy and alive as you have ever been. Flex your muscles and stretch and move, and enjoy your perfect self.

Now it's time for breakfast. Will you eat at home or will you eat out?... Will you share this breakfast time with others? Now imagine the most perfect breakfast you could possibly have... what will you eat?

It's time now for work. Will you work where you live or will you go somewhere to work? How will you get there?...

Now imagine that you have arrived at your workplace. Look around you. It is the perfect place for you to work. Are you outside or inside? Are their people? Animals? Plants? Machines? Technology? Tools? Books? Art? ...

Are you creating, leading, teaching, guiding, repairing, presenting, expressing your ideas, arranging, crafting, driving, flying, riding, engaging in a sport, performing, serving, persuading, analyzing, reading, meditating, inventing?....

What is your favorite part of your work?

Appendix 1

The morning is over, and you're hungry! What will you do for lunch? This is the most perfect lunch you have ever had... will it be with others or alone? Where will you eat? What will you have?....

After lunch, will you do the same tasks as you did in the morning, or will your day change? What is the first thing you do? Where are you?

The time flies by, because you are having a wonderful time. You are doing what you love the most, and you are feeling challenged, excited, and happy. What are you doing that makes you feel so good?

It's late afternoon now. How will you make the transition from work to relaxation, rest, or recreation? Will you spend time on your own, or will you see family or friends?

Imagine now it is almost evening and you are at home. Walk outside the place you live and look at it. Walk all around the building. Do you live in an apartment, a condo, a house, a motor home, an RV, a cabin... where do you live?

Walk inside. Is there anyone there? Family or friends? Pets?

Go to your favorite room. What is it like? Upstairs or downstairs? What are the colors?

Now you are hungry for dinner. What will you do for dinner? Will you eat at home or elsewhere? Alone or with others? It is the most perfect dinner of your life, so

Appendix 1

imagine the place and the atmosphere and then, what it is you are eating....

What will you do after dinner? Will you rest, or are there other activities? On this most beautiful evening, what will you do?

It is getting late, and you are deliciously tired. Go to a window or doorway and look outside. Can you see the stars from where you live? Look up at the stars and think about this perfect day. What was it about this day that was so right? How did you feel about yourself? How do you feel about the future?

Now you are ready for bed... slip into the most wonderful sleeping clothes and then quietly go to your soft and lovely bed. As you fall asleep, again there are lights circling around you, and you realize that the time machine has come to take you back to the past.
With a fond farewell to the future, you are now swept back to the past.

It is Two Thousand and ____. Two Thousand and ____. Two Thousand and ____....
(*and so on until it is the present year.*) You are waking up at our workshop!
Slowly open your eyes and sit up.

Let's share our perfect days...

Appendix 2
The Mentoring Interview

The mentoring interview pulls all the information together from the individual assessments and the group activities. The purposes of the interview are:

1. To build a relationship that has the potential for a long term correspondence;
2. To give the young woman accurate feedback about her interests, personality characteristics, and values:
3. To focus on building strengths and resolving risk issues; and
4. To set goals for the future.

In addition, the mentor should accomplish the following:

1. Make each young woman feel special and unique.
2. Compare each young woman to an eminent woman whose personality is similar to hers.
3. Help each young woman to have hope for the future
4. Let the young woman do most of the talking
5. Help her to make her career decisions based on her most deeply held values
6. Conduct the interview and the interpretations of assessments within the context of each young woman's culture.

The following script will provide a 1 – 1 ½ hour interview.

Appendix 2

Part 1 Greeting and Introduction

Greet the mentee in a culturally appropriate way, using quiet time, warmth, and distance, and eye contact that is comfortable for her. Introduce yourself with first name and last name, and stress that she can use your first name. Ask open ended questions and use verbal following to ask how she is feeling today and her responses to the workshop so far.

How is school going for you? What do you like best and least about it?
How is your family situation right now?
Can you tell me a little about your friendships and relationships?
How have your school, family, and friends supported you emotionally and academically?

Part 2 Goals and Visions

What career goals have you considered?
What was happening in your Perfect Future Day Fantasy?
What does your fantasy say about your goals?

Part 3. Interpretation of Assessments

In interpreting the instruments, go from the broadest categories to the most specific. Start with the Vocational Preference Inventory, then the Personality Research Form, then the Values Inventory.

Let's look at your VPI. The VPI is a sort of personality test that compares your responses with those of thousands of other people who have taken the test. Your three letter code tells you just what kinds of environments you would be happiest in – where you would find people like yourself and do things you enjoy. (Give further explanation and show the Holland Hexagon).

Your top three letter code is _____.

That's really neat! The kinds of people who have those codes are _____, _____, and _____.

If this fits her career goals, let her know that she is already really good at understanding the world of work and herself. If it doesn't fit, and she is very committed to those goals, then tell how it is possible for a person with a different personality to make it in that field. "Often the people who bring about change in a field are those who are a little different from the others!" If she is not very committed to her initial goals, encourage her to consider these possible vocations.
Most of the women are science oriented, therefore, help the mentee to see how her personality code fits within STEM professions.

Would you like to read this description? What do you think of it? How is it like you or not like you?

Now let's look at the PRF. This is an instrument that compares your needs as they are right now with lots of other people who have taken this test. For each of these scores, there is a way to turn a personality need into a strength – or in some cases, it's something in yourself you might need to overcome to get where you want to go.

Appendix 2

Your three highest scores are _____, _____, _____.

Would you like to read the description? What do you think this means for you?
Can you give examples from your own life that fit this pattern of needs?

Your lowest scores are _____,,_____, and _____.

That means you don't have much need for these things. What do you think about that?

Now let's put together the two tests, and see how your personality can help you achieve your career goals. (Synthesize the two tests, and see if you can create a profile that matches a famous woman or a woman in a popular books or movies).
Now let's look at your values. You ranked _____, _____, and _____ as your highest values. What do each of these values mean to you? How are they precious to you?

Do you see any ways that the career goals that we have talked about can help you to fulfill these values? Or do you need to rearrange your goals a little so that your values can be preserved?

Most eminent women are people who make their decisions based on their most deeply held values, as well as their strengths of character and intellect. If you make your decision based on what you really need and care about and value, you'll be more likely to achieve your dreams.

Appendix 2

Part 3 Risk Assessment

What barriers do you see inside yourself and in your world that could prevent you from achieving your goals?
In the risk group, what kinds of personal behaviors put you at risk for losing your dreams?
What would you like to do about these aspects of yourself? How could you get the support you need to change these things?
(Offer suggestions of ways to help change internal barriers).

What barriers are there in your family, school, and relationships to your goals?
What would you like to do about these? How can you get the help you need?
(Offer suggestions of resources. Money is the major issue brought up; give her the scholarship resources and reassure her that there are many ways to get to college and to pay for it.)

Part 4 Personal Map of the Future

The last thing we will do together is to put all of this information together to create a Personal Map of the Future. (Show the Map).
On this Map, you'll write what you need to do today, tomorrow, this week, and this month to achieve your goal. So write at least one goal at the top.

Appendix 2

Now, what can you do today? (Discuss, and remind her that she has already taken the first step by coming to this workshop.)
What about tomorrow? (Suggest visits to the career library, the counselor, the Web)
What about next week? (Suggest ordering information, applying for admissions tests, etc)
What about next month?
Next year?
Future steps?
Great! You have a wonderful map of your future!

Part 5 Leave taking

Express your enjoyment and affection. "This interview was so special! What I liked best was your _____."

Ask for any further questions.

Assure her that you will write her if she writes you, and exchange emails or addresses.

Let her know that the program is here for her, as well as ASU, to help her in the future, and that she will always be welcome. Wish her luck!

Appendix 2

NAME: _____

DEMOGRAPHICS

1. Age: _____   2. Grade: _____

3. What is your ethnic background?

____African American   _____Asian

____Hispanic/Latino   ____ Native American

(Tribe?_____)

____Caucasian   ____Other

(pleasespecify)_____

4. Household Information:
A. Does your father live in your home?
____Yes   ____No

B. Does your mother live in your home?

____Yes   ____No

C. Do any other adults live in your home?

____Yes   ____No

If yes, what is their relationship with you?

_____   _____

D. Number of children in your family, including you: _____

 E. Do you have a brother who has attended

college?   ____Yes   ____No

Appendix 2

F. Do you have a sister who has attended college?

____Yes ____No

5. Is your father currently employed?
____Yes ____No   If yes, what does he do?

_____

6. What is your father's level of completed education? ___ some grade school

____8th grade ____high school/GED

____some college or technical training

____2-year College ____College

____Graduate School

7. Is your mother currently employed?
____Yes ____No   If yes, what does she do?

_____

8. What is your mother's level of completed

education? ____ some grade school

____8th grade ___high school/GED

____some college or technical training
____2-year College ____College
____Graduate School

9. What is your religion? ___Catholic ____Jewish
____Mormon ____Protestant

Appendix 2

____Tribal Religion (which one?)

_____

____Other (which one?)

_____

10. Do you work? ____Yes ____No   If yes,
how many hours per week? _____

11. Are you active in extracurricular activities?
____Yes ____No   If yes, which ones?

_____

12. What high school math courses have you
taken? (including ones you're in now)

_____

13. What high school science courses have you
taken? (including ones you're in now)

_____

Appendix 3

MEASURES

CAREER EXPLORATION ACTIVITY INVENTORY

1. In the past <u>two months</u>, have you visited the school career library or library and read any of the materials pertaining to careers?

_____Yes _____No

2. In the past <u>two months</u>, have you read about careers in places other than Career Services or the library?

_____Yes _____No

3. In the past <u>two months</u>, have you sent for materials pertaining to careers?

_____Yes _____No

4. In the past <u>two months</u>, have you spoken to any of the following people about your career plans?

School counselors _____Yes _____No

Teachers _____Yes _____No

Parents _____Yes _____No

Other family members _____Yes _____No

Friends _____Yes _____No

People working in the field ____Yes _____No

Other _____Yes _____No

Appendix 3

5. If you could accomplish any career goal you wanted to, what would be your ideal career?

    Not Very   Very

  a. How committed are you to this career goal?
      1   2   3   4   5   6   7

  b. How important is this career goal to you?
      1   2   3   4   5   6   7

6. What is a career goal you think might be obtainable or realistic for you?

    Not Very   Very

  a. How committed are you to this career goal?
      1   2   3   4   5   6   7

  b. How important is this career goal to you?
      1   2   3   4   5   6   7

7. What do you see as the major obstacles to you achieving your career goals?

Appendix 4
EDUCATIONAL SELF-EFFICACY SCALE

Job Questionnaire
Instructions: For each job, circle the number that shows how confident (sure) you are that, if you really wanted to, you could finish the education (training) to enter that job.

How confident (sure) are you that you could finish the education (training) necessary for each job?

Job
Not sure   Moderately sure   Very sure

1. Retail florist
    1   2   3   4   5   6   7
2. Shipping and receiving clerk
    1   2   3   4   5   6   7
3. Chemist
    1   2   3   4   5   6   7
4. High school principal
    1   2   3   4   5   6   7
5. Fashion store manager
    1   2   3   4   5   6   7
6. Painter/artist
    1   2   3   4   5   6   7
7. Dentist
    1   2   3   4   5   6   7
8. Airplane pilot
    1   2   3   4   5   6   7
9. Nurse practitioner
    1   2   3   4   5   6   7

Appendix 4
Job

Not sure   Moderately sure   Very sure

10. Newspaper editor
     1   2   3   4   5   6   7
11. Stockbroker
     1   2   3   4   5   6   7
12. Secretary
     1   2   3   4   5   6   7
13. Veterinarian
     1   2   3   4   5   6   7
14. Speech therapist
     1   2   3   4   5   6   7
15. Mechanical engineer
     1   2   3   4   5   6   7
16. Public relations rep.
     1   2   3   4   5   6   7
17. Accountant
     1   2   3   4   5   6   7
18. Law enforcement officer
     1   2   3   4   5   6   7
19. Psychologist
     1   2   3   4   5   6   7
20. Car salesperson
     1   2   3   4   5   6   7
21. Nutritionist/dietician
     1   2   3   4   5   6   7
22. Actor/director
     1   2   3   4   5   6   7
23. Computer operator
     1   2   3   4   5   6   7
24. Travel agent
     1   2   3   4   5   6   7
25. Forester
     1   2   3   4   5   6   7

Appendix 4
Job

26. Elementary teacher

      1   2   3   4   5   6   7

27. Architect

      1   2   3   4   5   6   7

28. Financial analyst

      1   2   3   4   5   6   7

29. Interior designer

      1   2   3   4   5   6   7

30. Professional athletic coach

      1   2   3   4   5   6   7

School Questionnaire

Instructions: For each of the school subjects listed below, circle the number that shows how confident (sure) you are that you could do well in that course or subject area.

How confident (sure) are you that you could finish each of these courses with an A or a B?

Course

Not sure   Moderately sure   Very sure

31. General math

      1   2   3   4   5   6   7

32. Business math

      1   2   3   4   5   6   7

33. Algebra

      1   2   3   4   5   6   7

34. Geometry

      1   2   3   4   5   6   7

35. Advanced math   (trigonometry, calculus)

      1   2   3   4   5   6   7

Appendix 4

Course

Not sure			Moderately sure			Very sure

36. Earth science

1   2   3   4   5   6   7

37. Life science

1   2   3   4   5   6   7

38. Biology

1   2   3   4   5   6   7

39. Chemistry

1   2   3   4   5   6   7

40. Physics

1   2   3   4   5   6   7

41. American History

1   2   3   4   5   6   7

42. US Government

1   2   3   4   5   6   7

43. English

1   2   3   4   5   6   7

School Questionnaire: Part 2

How confident (sure) are you that you could get mostly A's and B's in the following subject areas?
(NOTE: NE = means that you are NOT ENROLLED in this course this year)

Course

Not sure			Moderately sure			Very sure

44. Math *this* year

1   2   3   4   5   6   7   NE

45. Math *throughout high*   *school*1

1   2   3   4   5   6   7   NE

46. English *this year*

1   2   3   4   5   6   7   NE

Appendix 4

Course

Not sure   Moderately sure   Very sure

47. English *throughout high school*

     1   2   3   4   5   6   7   NE

48. Social studies *this year*

     1   2   3   4   5   6   7   NE

49. Social studies *throughout high school*

     1   2   3   4   5   6   7   NE

50. Science *this year*

     1   2   3   4   5   6   7   NE

51. Science *throughout high school*

     1   2   3   4   5   6   7   NE

Questions About Your Future

Part 1

Instructions: Please circle the number that best reflects your feelings about each statement.

Course

Not sure   Moderately sure   Very sure

52. How sure are you that you will have a job when you get older?

     1   2   3   4   5   6   7

53. If you plan to work, do you know what you would like to do when you get older?

     1   2   3   4   5   6   7

54. How sure are you that you will graduate from high school?

     1   2   3   4   5   6   7

55. How sure are you that you will go on to college or some other type of training after high school?

     1   2   3   4   5   6   7

Appendix 4

What is your favorite school subject?

_____

What school subject do you like least?

_____

Part 2

Instructions: Please circle the number that best reflects your feelings about each statement.

How much do you agree or disagree with each of these statements?

Statement
Disagree a lot   Not sure   Agree a lot

56. Finish high school will help me get a good job.
    1 2 3 4 5 6 7
57. Finishing my high school education is very important to me.
    1 2 3 4 5 6 7
58. Going on to college is very important to me.
    1 2 3 4 5 6 7
59. Finishing high school probably will not make much difference in the kind of job I get.
    1 2 3 4 5 6 7
60. Finishing college will help me get a good job.
    1 2 3 4 5 6 7
61. Finishing college will help me get the job I really want.
    1 2 3 4 5 6 7
62. I haven't really thought much about what job I really want.
    1 2 3 4 5 6 7

Appendix 4

Statement

Disagree a lot   Not sure   Agree a lot

63. I will not have to work when I get older.

     1   2   3   4   5   6   7

64. How I do in school really doesn't matter very much.

     1   2   3   4   5   6   7

65. How well I do in school will make a lot of difference in what kind of job I get.

     1   2   3   4   5   6   7

66. I have no idea what I want to do when I get out of school.

     1   2   3   4   5   6   7

67. I have been thinking a lot about what I want to do when I get out of school.

     1   2   3   4   5   6   7

68. Getting a good job is very important to me.

     1   2   3   4   5   6   7

69. Getting a job I really like is very important to me.

     1   2   3   4   5   6   7

70. Getting a job that pays well is very important to me.

     1   2   3   4   5   6   7

71. I like school a lot.

     1   2   3   4   5   6   7

72. How well I do in high school will make a lot of difference in my life.

     1   2   3   4   5   6   7

73. I plan to get married.

     1   2   3   4   5   6   7

74. I will not work after I am married.

     1   2   3   4   5   6   7

Appendix 5
Adolescent At-Risk Behaviors Inventory
Robinson (1992)

IMPORTANT: Circle only one answer for each question.

1. How do you think of yourself?
   a. very underweight
   b. slightly underweight
   c. about the right weight
   d. slightly overweight
   e. very overweight

2. How satisfied do you feel about the following specific parts of your body?

Not at all Satisfied   *Very Satisfied*

a. thighs

    1   2   3   4   5

b. buttocks

    1   2   3   4   5

c. hips

    1   2   3   4   5

d. stomach

    1   2   3   4   5

e. legs

    1   2   3   4   5

f. waist

    1   2   3   4   5

g. breasts

    1   2   3   4   5

h. upper arms

    1   2   3   4   5

i. lips

    1   2   3   4   5

Appendix 5

Not at all Satisfied   *Very Satisfied*

    j. hair

        1   2   3   4   5

    k. nose

        1   2   3   4   5

    l. skin tone

        1   2   3   4   5

3. Have you ever tried cigarette smoking, even one or two puffs?
    a. no
    a. yes
4. During the <u>past 30 days</u>, on how many days did you smoke cigarettes regularly?
    a. 0 days
    b. 1 or 2 days
    c. 3 to 5 days
    d. 6 to 9 days
    e. 10 to 19 days
    f. 20 to 29 days
    g. All 30 days

5. During the <u>past 30 days</u>, on the days you smoked, how many cigarettes did you smoke per day?
    a. I did not smoke cigarettes during the past 30 days
    b. Less than 1 cigarette per day
    c. 1 cigarette per day
    d. 2 to 5 cigarettes per day
    e. 6 to 10 cigarettes per day
    f. 11 to 20 cigarettes per day
    g. More than 20 cigarettes per day

Appendix 5

6. How old were you when you had sexual intercourse for the first time?
   a. I have never had sexual intercourse
   b. 17 years old or older
   c. 16 years old
   d. 15 years old
   e. 14 years old
   f. 13 years old
   g. less than 12 years old

7. Was your first sexual experience your choice?
   a. I have never had sexual intercourse
   b. Yes
   c. No

8. How often do you drink alcohol or use drugs before you have sexual intercourse?
   a. I have never had sexual intercourse
   b. Never
   c. Seldom
   d. Frequently
   e. Always

9. The last time you had sexual intercourse, did you or your partner use a condom?
   a. I have never had sexual intercourse
   b. Yes
   c. No

10. The last time you had sexual intercourse, what one method did you or your partner use to prevent pregnancy? (Select only one response.)
    a. I have never had sexual intercourse
    b. Birth Control pills
    c. Condoms

d. Some other method (which one?)_____
e. Withdrawal
f. Not sure
g. No method was used to prevent pregnancy

11. During the <u>past month,</u> how many times have you used alcohol?
    a. I don't drink
    b. 1-4 times (once a week or less)
    c. 5-7 times (more than once a week but less than twice a week)
    d. 8-12 times (two or three times a week)
    e. More than three times a week

12. During the <u>past year,</u> how many times have you used alcohol?
    a. I don't drink
    b. 1-4 times (once every three months)
    c. 5-11 times (once every couple of months)
    d. 12-24 times (once or twice per month)
    e. 25 times or more (once or more every week)

13. How much alcohol do your friends drink on average?
    a. My friends don't drink alcohol
    b. 1-4 times a year (once every three months)
    c. 5-11 times (once every couple of months)
    d. 12-24 times (once or twice per month)

e. 25 times or more (once or more every week)

14. During the <u>past month</u>, how many times have you used marijuana?
    a. I don't use marijuana
    b. 1-4 times (once a week or less)
    c. 5-7 times (more than once a week but less than twice a week)
    d. 8-12 times (two or three times a week)
    e. More than three times a week

15. During the <u>past year</u>, how many times have you used marijuana?
    a. I haven't used marijuana in the past year
    b. 1-4 times a year (once every three months)
    c. 5-11 times a year (once every couple of months)
    d. 12-24 times a year (once or twice per month)
    e. 25 times or more a year (more than twice a month)

17. During the <u>past month</u>, how many times have you used any other drug, such as ecstasy, mushrooms, speed, ice, heroin, or pills without a doctor's prescription?
    a. 0 times
    b. 1 or 2 times
    c. 3 to 9 times
    d. 10 to 19 times
    e. 20 to 39 times
    f. 40 or more times

18. During the past year, how many times have you used any other drug, such as ecstasy, mushrooms, speed, ice, heroin, or pills without a doctor's prescription?
    a. 0 times
    b. 1 or 2 times
    c. 3 to 9 times
    d. 10 to 19 times
    e. 20 to 39 times
    f. 40 or more times

Sometimes people feel as depressed and hopeless about the future that they may consider attempting suicide that is, taking some action to end their own life.

19. During the past month, did you ever seriously consider attempting suicide?
    a. no
    b. yes

20. During the past year, did you ever seriously consider attempting suicide?
    a. no
    b. yes

21. During the past month, did you make a plan about how you would attempt suicide?
    a. no
    b. yes

22. During the past year, did you make a plan about how you would attempt suicide?
    a. no
    b. yes

Appendix 5

23. During the <u>past month</u>, how many times did you actually attempt suicide?
    a. 0 times
    b. 1 time
    c. 2 or 3 times
    d. 4 or 5 times
    e. 6 or more times

24. During the <u>past year</u>, how many times did you actually attempt suicide?
    a. 0 times
    b. 1 time
    c. 2 or 3 times
    d. 4 or 5 times
    e. 6 or more times

25. If you attempted suicide during the <u>past year</u>, did any attempt result in an injury, poisoning, or overdose that had to be treated by a doctor or nurse?
    a. I did not attempt suicide during the past 12 months
    b. no
    c. yes

26. Have you been asked to join a gang?
    a. no
    b. yes

27. If you are a member of a gang right now, how long have you been a member?
    a. I don't belong to a gang.
    b. 0-3 months
    c. 3-6 months
    d. 6-12 months

e. 1-2 years
f. 2-3 years
g. 3+ years

28. If in a gang, were you recruited by a:
    a. I don't belong to a gang
    b. parent
    c. brother
    d. sister
    e. cousin
    f. aunt/uncle
    g. friend
    h. acquaintance
    i. stranger

29. If you are in a gang, do you want to remain a member?
    a. I don't belong to one.
    b. No
    c. Yes

30. If you wanted to leave the gang, how difficult would it be for you to leave?
    a. I don't belong to a gang
    b. Very easy
    c. Easy
    d. Somewhat difficult
    e. Very difficult

31. Have you ever tried to leave the gang to which you presently belong?
    a. I don't belong to a gang
    b. Yes
    c. No

Appendix 5

32. The most important reason you belong to a gang is (please pick one only):
    a. I don't belong to a gang
    b. protection for myself
    c. protection for my family
    d. friendship
    e. being around people who understand who I am
    f. to fit in
    g. Other_____

Appendix 6

Useful Links and Resources for Counseling Talented Girls and Women

http://www.ehr.nsf.gov/ehr/hrd/ge/gender-rev.html

http://www.nae.edu/NAE/CWE/cwemain.nsf/weblinks/KGRG-5DDHE5?

http://www.nagc.org/Publications/Parenting

http://www.aboutourkids.org/articles/giftedgirls.html

http://www.hoagiesgifted.org/gender.html

http://www.twicegifted.net/gender.html

http://www.ncpamd.com/gift_women.html

http://mathforum.org/library/view/8883.html

http://www.sp.uconn.edu/~nrcgt/news/spring01/sprng013.html

http://www.gifteddevelopment.com

http://www.sengifted.org/articles_

http://cfge.wm.edu/documents/GenderGenius.html

http://researchmag.asu.edu/stories/anidea.html

http://www.counselingthegifted.com/books.html

http://www.io.com/~redden/taglinks.html

Appendix 6

http://mensa76.us.mensa.org/Social-Dev-in-the-Gifted2002.html

lhttp://www.kidsource.com/kidsource/content/career_planning.html

http://www.roeperreview.org/resources/roeper.pdf

http://www.smu.edu/continuing_education/youth

http://www.jhu.edu/gifted/research/biblio.html

Index

A

American Association of
    University Women   *33,34,46*
Arnold, Karen   *34,39*

B

Benbow, Camilla   *65*

C

Campbell, P.   *20,47*
Career Counseling   *100-101*
Chang, J. C.   *45-46*
College Women   *45-85*
    Academic Persistence   *47-50*
    Career Goals   *69-70*
    College Environment   *62-64*
    Mentors   *70-71*
    Multipotentiality   *66-68*
    Risk Factors   *50-55*
    Self Beliefs   *55-59*
    STEM Majors   *47-50, 65-66*
Cohn, Sanford   *23,39*
Colangelo, Nicholas   *22,30,39,66*
Corrigan, Margret   *131-143*

D

Dannenbaum, Sandra   *109-129*
Development of Talent   *12-43*
    Culture of Romance   *31-34,54*
    Gender Gap   *19*
    Gender Socialization   *35*
    Inequity 31-34
    Self Esteem Plunge   *28-30*
    Sex Differences   *21-25*

E

Eccles, Jacqueline   *63,75,65*

F

Fielder, Katherine   *99-107*
Foley-Nicpon, Megan   *19-43*

G

GEOS   *165-199*
Gilligan, Carol   *111,129*

Index